Studies on Information Science and Tagore

By the same author

- **Knowledge Dissemination and Publication:** Tagore in the Perspective of Information Science
- **Tagore in Prints:** A Comparative Study Before and After Expiry of Copyright

---

About the Author

Partha Pratim Ray, M.A., M. Lib., I. Sc, M. Phil., Ph.D. in Library and Information Science is a working Deputy Librarian and in-charge Institute of Agriculture Library, and Bangadesh Bhavana Library Visva-Bharati. He has teaching experience of more than twelve years in undergraduate and post-graduate level at different universities. Dr. Ray has contributed more than forty-one research papers in journals of national and international repute and chapters to nine books. Besides Tagore's literature (Tagoreana) his area of specialization includes information communication in society, copyright and bibliometric study. Dr. Ray is the author of the books entitled: *Tagore in Print: A Comparative Study Before and After Expiry of Copyright (2012); Knowledge Dissemination and Publication: Tagore in the Perspective of Information Science (2014)* with Prof. B. K. Sen.

Studies on Information Science and Tagore

Partha Pratim Ray

CONCEPT PUBLISHING COMPANY PVT. LTD.
NEW DELHI-110059

ISBN-13: 978-93-86682-67-3

First Published in 2018

Published and Printed by

Concept Since 1974

Concept Publishing Company Pvt. Ltd.
A/15-16, Commercial Block, Mohan Garden,
New Delhi-110059 (INDIA)
T : 91 11 25351460, 91 11 25351794
E : publishing@conceptpub.com; *W* : www.conceptpub.com

Cataloging in Publication Data--Courtesy: D.K. Agencies (P) Ltd. <docinfo@dkagencies.com>

Ray, Partha Pratim, author.
Studies on information science and Tagore / Partha Pratim Ray.
pages cm
Includes bibliographical references and index.
ISBN 9789386682673

1. Information science--India. 2. Tagore, Rabindranath, 1861-1941--Criticism and interpretation. 3. Bengali literature--Publishing. 4. Copyright--India. I. Title.

LCC Z665.2.I4R39 2018 DDC 020.954 23

To my children Antara and Pitam
My ultimate motivators
My world of joy and laughter

Preface

Library Science is an interdisciplinary evolving subject along with different areas of library like collection, organization, preservation, and dissemination of information. Among many other subjects it incorporates management, information communication technology and education. Collection and dissemination of processed information through different tools and techniques is the central focus of library as its product and services. That is why it is termed as library and information science, bibliothecography, information studies so on. Shiyali Ramamrita Ranganathan (1892-1972) known as father of Library Science in India had dedicated his life for the cause of development of library, library profession and library science as a discipline. He has made good number of unmatched fundamental thought provoking contributions in library science like Five Laws of Library Science, Colon Classification, Classified Catalogue Code, Chain Indexing to name few. Dr. Ranganathan has provided scientific as well as philosophical basis, not only of the subject but also of the profession.

Rabindranath Tagore (1861-1941) though popularly known as a poet, but Bengali literature in particular and world literature in general has been enriched by his creation in all literary forms like poetry, dramatic works, songs, essays, novels, travelogue, short stories. Tagore's published verse and dramas amount to one lakh fifty thousand lines. His non-dramatic works is more than twice as much. Tagore's fame as a poet over-shadowed his great contributions to other fields of literature that deserves more attention and appreciation. Besides his literary creation he was an editor, dramatist, social, political, religious reformer, aesthetic thinker, educational innovator, pioneer of rural reconstruction in India, a cultural ambassador. The University of Oxford while conferring the degree *D. litt. honoris causa* on Tagore in 1940 has rightly mentioned "Here before you is the myriad-minded poet and writer" (*'poeta et scriptor myrianous')*.

Tagore's vision on society, religion, aesthetics, education, rural reconstruction, nationalism, internalism has been reflected in his numerous writings. Tagore started drawing and painting at the age of sixty seven, yet achieved distinction as a painter. Tagore's concept on library has also been reflected in his numerous writing of all literary forms which covers both philosophical as well as functional aspect of library. All the intellectual creations of Rabindranath can be termed as Tagoreana. Based on Ranganathan and Tagore's philosophy of library, applications of different theories of library science for information-communication, social need as well as to draw creative portrait of total creation of scholars like Rabindranath Tagore, Satyajit Ray, post-copyright publications scenario of Tagoreana the present work is divided into two segments—Information Science and Tagoreana.

Studies on Information Science

S.R. Ranganathan formulated Five Laws of Library Science are considered as bedrock of Library Science. Ranganathan conceived the idea of five laws of library science in 1928. The Laws appeared in book form in 1931. Five laws of Library Science formulated by S.R. Ranganathan have great impact on library, library science and library profession. Rabindranath Tagore also expressed his vision of library, its services, philosophy in his numerous writings in different literary forms. The paper *"Ranganathan's five laws and Tagore's vision of library: A study"* highlights that central focus of both the thinkers are to maximize use of library collection for social benefit. Tagore expressed it in his poetic language, whereas Ranganathan with the help of laws, canons etc. Tagore's vision of library is based on his educational philosophy.

Shiyali Ramamrita Ranganathan, father of Library Science in India paves the way of establishing Library Science as social science and librarianship as a profession with his dedicated efforts and intellectual bent of mind. He has originated a good number of classical theories and their practical applications too with rules, regulations, laws, canons etc. Philosophical foundation is the basis for establishment of any discipline or profession. The paper entitled *"Influence of Manu on Ranganathan's Philosophy of Library Science: An Overview"* is an attempt to trace out the influencing philosophical factor which laid the philosophical foundation in his mind for lifelong academic and professional persuasion. It helps to conclude that Laws of *Manu* known as *Manu Samhita* or *Manusmriti* has a great influence on Ranganathan's thoughts in particular and Indian classical epic literature in general.

Information is considered as one of the most powerful instrument for bringing about socio-economic development on egalitarian line. After Independence Government of India has undertaken various measures for increase of literacy among the people, especially for Scheduled Caste and Scheduled Tribe communities and to make them educate, aware about the need and importance for information, knowledge for development. The study *"Information for Tribal Development: A Case Study of Santals—Attitude and Adjustment"* is an attempt to examine whether three successive generations of the primitive community, the Santals, living in close proximity with the educated and cultured environment of Visva-Bharati, Santiniketan (India) have brought about any change in their attitude towards education in general and information in particular. It is observed from the study that there is no significance of difference of attitude generation-wise towards information.

Marriage acts as foundation of society through social and legal union of men and women. In social marriage socio-economic choice plays a pivotal role. Among many other sources of disseminating information matrimonial advertisements in newspapers serves as information sharing communication process in social marriage. In the article *"Matrimonial (Socio-economic) Choice and Bradford's Law: A Study"*, socio-economic choice of 600 each of bride and bridegroom in matrimonial advertisements in two leading Bengali newspapers *(Anandabazar* and *Bartaman Patrika)* were analysed. In marriage socio-economic choice plays a predominant role in selection of bride and bridegroom. The choices are many and vary from society to society, person to person. But there are some core choices. "Bradford's Law of Scattering" was applied to identify core choices of bride and bridegroom. It is observed from the study that first and second zone of socio-economic choice of both bride and bridegroom strictly follows Bradford law but marginally varies in third zone. This study may open new vistas of sociological research with the application of Bradford law.

The paper entitled *"Creativity of Satyajit Ray: A Bibliometric Portrait"* is an effort to sketch productivity output of *Bharat Ratna,* Oscar winner Satyajit Ray, as a film-maker and literary personality with the help of bibliometric technique. He has published 61 books during 1967-2002 of which 15 titles were published posthumously. Moreover, besides 39 screen-plays he has published 69 articles in English and 53 articles in Bengali on filmography as well as other topics. His productivity coefficient for books stands to 2.21; screen-plays 2.35; filmography 1.63; articles in English 1.41 and Bengali stands to 1.71. On the other hand publication density of articles in English and Bengali are 2.30 and 2.21 respectively. Ray has published 69 articles in English in 30 channels and 53 articles in Bengali in 24 channels leading to publication concentration 23.33 and 16.67 respectively.

Tagoreana

Rabindranath gave copyright of all his intellectual output to his creation Visva-Bharati. Accordingly, Visva-Bharati enjoyed monopoly of Tagore's copyright. But the copyright period ended in December 2001. In the post-copyright scenario private publishers are free to publish Tagoreana (Tagore's literature). In the paper entitled *"Publications of Tagoreana before after Expiry of Copyright: A Study"* an attempt has been made to find out trend, type and number of publications of Tagoreana by private publishers. A comparison has also been made in respect of price, number and size of pages of books published by Visva-Bharati and private publishers. It is observed from the study that a very small portion of publishers publishing a meagre number of commercially viable titles of Tagoreana with less price but poor quality of paper, printing comparison to Visva-Bharati. Private publishers published Tagoreana with less number of pages to keep the price low.

In the post-copyright phase private publishers are publishing basically commercially viable titles of Tagoreana at low cost. It raises the question how far uniqueness or qualities of his writings are maintained by publishers of all sorts, particularly in case of impression, composition, font size etc. The paper on *"Post Copyright Publication of Tagorean Fiction: A Study"* attempts to find out the quality of post-copyright publication of Tagorean fiction by private publishers in respect of punctuation marks changed or omitted, additional punctuation mark used, other mistakes such as spelling, words, sentences, paragraph clubbed or deleted etc. along with comparative price and size with Visva-Bharati publications. It is observed that a good number of Bengali publishers are publishing Tagorean fiction. The prices of these books are lower than Visva-Bharati publications, but are of poor quality in respect of paper, binding, impression as well as with huge number of mistakes.

The paper *"Painting and Drawings of Rabindranath Tagore: An Analytical Study"* attempts to study 1573 numbers of Tagore's paintings and drawings kept in Rabindra-Bhavana, Visva-Bharati, with the help of bibliometric technique and found that Rabindranath drawn paintings in different places and dates, on different themes, medium, canvases and also put various kinds of signature on different positions of the paintings. It is observed that Rabindranath composed a good number of drawings and paintings in a short span of 12 years (15.3.1929-3.11.1940) on different themes, with various colour combinations. As subject Rabindranath's paintings include figure in different shapes and forms, human face, head study, landscape, birds, animals, nude etc. Every subject has its own childlike imaginary rhythmic specialty.

The paper *"Rabindranath Tagore: A Bibliometric Portrait"* highlights the publication productivity of Rabindranath Tagore. He has published 199 Bengali books during 1878-1941 and 36 titles were published posthumously making it 235 Bengali books to his credit. In his seventies (the last decade of his life), when he ventured into the world of painting, surprisingly his literary productivity increased considerably instead of going down. He published as many as 55 books apart from producing 2000 + paintings. Tagore's productivity encompassed all branches of literature, i.e. poems, dramas, letters, novels, essays, songs, travelogues, comedies, short stories, addresses, textbooks and autobiography. His productivity coefficient for Bengali books is 0.84 which indicates that he had a steady publication record throughout his literary career. He has published 91 out of 95 short stories in 16 communication channels Publication density of short stories is 5.69, publication concentration is 12.5 and productivity coefficient for short stories stands at 0.32.

Partha Pratim Ray

Acknowledgements

This book would not have been seen the light of the day without support and encouragement of several persons and institutions. It is difficult to express my gratitude to all of them by name. Yet, firstly, I would like to express my sincere gratitude to my mentor Professor B.K. Sen, Chairman, Expert Committee on Bibliometrics, Department of Science & Technology, Government of India and Member, Research Council on History of Science, Indian National Science Academy, a scholar, philosopher and humanist who led me into the world of Tagore. Applications of bibliometric laws to the creation of literary personality like Rabindranath would not have been possible without his continuous encouragement, keen interest and valuable guidance.

The author also acknowledges academicians, friends and colleagues who have helped me in this journey through their criticism and valuable comments. To name few I would like to mention those with whom I interacted and enriched at various academic forums, Prof. Juran Krishna Sarkhel, Dr. Bablu Sutradhar, Prof. Krishnapada Majumder, Dr. Parthasarathi Mukhopadhyay, Dr. V. K. Thomas, Dr. Sabuj Kumar Chaudhury. I am really thankful to you!

I am specially obliged to various libraries of Visva-Bharati library system that provided support and allowed me to access their resources. Particularly to the Curator and the staff-members of the Archives, Library as well as Audio-Visual section, Tagorean Research Centre Rabindra-Bhavana, Visva-Bharati.

Last but not the least, the author is thankful to his family members mother Sunity Ray, wife Bani, kids Antara and Pitam for their moral support and sacrifice of leisure without which the work would not have been possible.

A tribute goes out to Tagore's creation **Santiniketan** *(Where the world makes its home in a single nest)* which, through its ability to create an atmosphere of freedom of mind, freedom of heart and freedom of will and love for nature lifted my spirit for creative thinking.

Santiniketan **Partha Pratim Ray**
Ist January, 2018

Contents

SECTION I

Studies on Information Science

1

Ranganathan's Five Laws and Tagore's Vision of Library

A Study

Introduction

Shiyali Ramamrita Ranganathan (1892-1972) known as father of Library Science in India had dedicated his life for the cause of development of library, library profession and library science in India. His relentless planned work, collecting ideas or instances to formulate theories, principles or policies, ploughback the solution to work, writing papers and interacting with contemporary research made him known as father of library science in India and librarian to the world. It is basically one man created movement that has established the profession in India. The American Library Association paid tribute to Ranganathan as "Your words are the words of the Anglo-American, but your language is the language of the East and your ideas are universal. You answer the challenge of the future with a challenge. Most of us are not your disciples; all of us are your students. For a generation you have forced librarians to think. We are proud to be in your debt."[1] He has made numerous fundamental contributions in different areas of library science like classification and indexing, cataloguing in the form—Colon Classification, Classified Catalogue Code, Chain Indexing, library organization, management, administration to name few. Through Five Laws of Library Science, Dr. Ranganathan has provided scientific as well as philosophical basis, not only of the subject but also of the profession. Ranganathan conceived the ideas of five laws of library science in 1928. He described the laws as fundamental laws in Normative Principles of Library Science and appeared in book form in 1931.[2]

Rabindranath Tagore (1861-1941) popularly known as poet, but he was a dramatist, writer of short stories, novelist, philosopher, composer and singer, innovator in education and rural development, actor, director, painter, cultural ambassador of India to the world. Rabindranath, writer of two National anthems (India and Bangladesh) composed first poem at the age of eight and by the end of his life, had written over twenty-five volumes of poetry, fifteen plays, ninety five short stories, eleven novels, thirteen volumes of essays, initiated and edited journals, made more than four thousand correspondence, composed over two thousand songs; created more than two thousand pictures and sketches.[3] His writings on literature, music, art, education, co-operative ideas, methods of knowledge and its communication all are relevant even today. Tagore never wrote any treatise on education, but his ideas on education can be traced out from his numerous writings in different literary forms, like poetry, essays, addresses, letters etc. Likewise, Tagore's vision on 'library' reflected in his numerous writings in different literary forms provides functional as well as philosophical foundations of the subject and profession.[4]

Objectives of the Study

- To understand Tagore's vision of library.
- To assess relevance of Tagore's vision of library with Ranganathan's five laws of library science.
- To understand Tagore's vision of library in the context of his educational philosophy.

Five Laws and Tagorean Vision of Library

Books are for Use: The stress of the first law is on the care of collection to invite and promote the maximum use of library collection. According to Tagore "The part of its contents which is for the purpose of extensive accumulation has its usefulness, but the other part which is for constant and varied use, gives its significance."[5] Tagore warned librarians to be free from bias of the number of accumulating as "greed is one of the chief man's internal enemies. Once he starts to gather and store, he becomes distracted with the obsession of number, and tends to overlook the purpose of his accumulating."[6] For better use of library collection documentation is necessary. Rabindranath suggested "it is necessary that its contents should be clearly and specifically brought to notice. Otherwise it is very difficult for the ordinary man to find his way about them, and the library is left as a city of vast accommodation that lacks means of communication."[7] Rabindranath in his poem has mentioned that books may be kept in precious racks with good care, but without proper use it is meaningless.[8]

For developing readership in a library Rabindranath reminds that the readers make the library is not the whole truth; but library also makes readers. For this, library has to go beyond the traditional form of invitation "Here is my catalogue, come and select for yourself. But in the usual catalogue there is no introduction, no invitation, and no spirit of welcome. That library alone can be called hospitable, which shows an eagerness to invite readers to the feast at its disposal, it is such hospitability that makes a library big not its size."[9] Ranganathan put forward same kind of opinion "...a library, keen about its books being fully used, will plant itself in the midst of its clientele."[10]

Books to be used at present and future generations to come it have to be preserved. One of the most important functions of a library is conservation of library collection to keep the documents safe from harm or loss, damage, destruction or decay, and maintain it in reasonably sound condition for present and future use. Rabindranath in his two poems *Kiter Bichar* and *Granthakit*[11] describes the nature of *kit* (worm) and how they destroy book. In the objectives and functions of *Santiniketan Brahmacharyashrama*, it is stated that the responsibility of cleaning the library, rooms and garden should be vested to students. Clear instruction was given to collect borrowed books from the guests.[12] In a letter to Subodh Chandra Majumder, Rabindranath's care for book is reflected. Where Rabindranath wrote "I mailed two books *Religious Systems* and *Origin of Aryans*. Keep them in the library. Dust the library and give naphthalene."[13]

Every Reader His Book and Every Book Its Reader: The Second and Third laws focus on the user and usable items. These laws try to make provision for *"books for all"* and resemble first law. But to ensure fullest use of its resources Tagore suggests, "it is necessary that its contents should clearly and specifically brought to notice" of readers with human touch because "the library by itself imposes a responsibility—the responsibility relating to riches. In so far as the library contains books, it attains fulfilment only through having those books read. It will not remain inactive; may it play an active role by issuing a call. Because *'Jannastam yanna diyate'* that which is not given is wasted.[14] For proper implementation of these laws book selection has a pivotal role to play. Regarding book selection Tagore suggests "... select books, not one of which is their only as an offerings of worship to Number, but each one which stands on its own merits."[15] In the same tone Ranganathan regarding "judgement of choice" mentioned "As a matter of fact, it may even be said that it is not so much to the size of the library as to the choice of its collections that the Second Law looks for the fulfilment of its message."[16]

A good book is a good friend that helps to know many unknown things, character building and also helps to develop creativity. Besides, it provides many information as it is not possible to go everywhere to observe everything. This concept has been reflected in a poem *Janmadine.*[17] The role of a book as a friend with whom one can exchange ideas has been reflected in a letter of Rabindranath where he mentioned *Amiel's Journal* as an intimate friend.[18] Rabindranath was a voracious reader who became deeply involved with the character of the books he read as he mentioned in describing the episode of *Ramayana* reading in *Jivansmriti.*[19] A good book has a long-term impact on reader's mind like classical song. It has also been reflected in Rabindranath's poetry[20] as well as letters.[21] Good books help to generate new ideas to write new things as Rabindranath has mentioned being impressed by a book entitled *Chineman Letter.* Rabindranath wrote an essay on this.[22] Actually Rabindranath's literary culture starts with habit of reading as he mentioned in his autobiography *Jivansmriti.*[23]

For development of reading habit among school students Rabindranath suggested for rapid reading literature books in English, Sanskrit along with traditional step-by-step teaching methods in these subjects.[24] For this rapid reading on many subjects, library is the only place. Pramathanath Bisi recaptured his memory of Rabindranath's opinion about library that people can never be truly educated from colleges and teachers, on the other hand he should be the teacher of his own and library is the proper place of education as he learns many things only from huge reading in a library.[25] For development of personal reading Rabindranath also mentioned in his poem that one college student prepares a list of gifts for his beloved one where "recent fiction" and book of poem "printed on antique paper" gets it place.[26] The same kind of reference can also be cited from his famous novel *Naukadubi* where Akshay presented books to Hemnalini as gift.[27] Tagore in his first directly and specifically writings on education *'Siksar Herpher'* mentioned "...It is essential to read many other reference book to digest a textbook. Study with joy helps to develop reading skill; power of accept, power of thinking and also power of digest as a natural process."[28] Self-reading has a tremendous impact in Tagore's education thinking. Library is the right place for this kind of reading. It is the responsibility of library to make provision for books to every reader.

Save the Time of the Reader: The fourth law completely centres on the reader and the organization with the ultimate object of providing efficient through access to library resources. For proper implementation of this law librarian has a great role to play. As Tagore suggests, "the worth of a librarian I would gauge by his power of attracting and looking after such circle, of acting as the intermediary for an intimacy of relationship between the reader and the library."[29] Regarding librarian's duty Rabindranath reminds "...as to the books, the librarian's duty should not be confined to those that he can gather, but he must also keep himself acquainted with all those others that are published from time to time, subject by subject."[30]

A hospitable librarian with his positive attitude towards service can convert a causal user to regular one. "A library which makes just enough provision that can be placed before its guests for their delectation, with a librarian who has the qualities of a host, not a store-keeper."[31] This type of qualities is essential to fulfil the fourth law. Tagore expects libraries role as active like Russia and mentioned "their (Russia) museum is not passive like our library at Santiniketan but active."[32] Similarly, Ranganathan in his "The Five Laws of Library Science" mentioned "...it is the Library Staff that ultimately makes or mars a library."[33]

A Library is a Growing Organism: The fifth Law emphasizes that library posses the attributes of a living organism and growing organism can only survive. The law focused on the need for internal change than change in the environment itself. Tagore in his poetic language narrated it as "the growth of this school was the growth of my life and not of a mere carrying out of my doctrines, its ideals changed with the maturity like a ripening fruit that not only grows in its bulk and deepens in its colour, but undergoes change in the very quality of its inner pulp."[34] Ranganathan with his academic and professional bent of mind suggested considering both child as well as adult growth in the planning and implementation stage of library. He mentioned "The modesty with which library authorities under estimate the rate of growth of each of these factors is unimaginable... a far less pardonable thing is to set about organizing a library as if it would be stationary, as if neither the books, nor the readers, nor the staff would grow in number."[35]

Tagore was not a dreamer. He gave concrete shape of his ideas from the beginning of the *Santiniketan Ashrama*. The objective of development of education and library is clearly expressed in the trust deed, *"in pursuance of the need of enhancement of the quality of living in the Ashrama the trustees were empowered to establish a Brahmavidyalaya at Santiniketan and a library."*[36] Thus, the concept of library was from the very beginning a constituent of the *Santiniketan Ashrama*. Tagore wrote "The collection of our revered father's books was kept in one of the three rooms. We first looked after the proper preservation of books and manuscripts. What occupied our thoughts thereafter was where we could fix students' residence."[37] So, the growth of library goes side by side along with the growth of *Santiniketan Ashrama* to a central university of national importance.

Tagore's Educational Philosophy

Education means the full awakening of vitality. And vitality means constant progress towards genuine interests. The object of education is to give unity of truth. Tagore expressed his opinion as "it is my firm conviction that there is a connection between the education of the body and the education of the mind, between the activeness of the body and the activeness of the mind."[38] He further clarifies, "education is not merely imparting of information; man has not been born to carry a load of information; the purpose at the root of life has to be realized. The aim of education is to realize fully through knowledge and action the entire purpose of human life."[39] Tagore tried to assert in his words and works that education has its only meaning and object in freedom—freedom from ignorance about the laws of universe, and freedom from passion and prejudice in our communication with the human world. To narrate the objective of education Tagore demanded that "we have also to know well the mind and the nature of man; for the fundamental purpose of education is not merely to enrich our stock of knowledge, but to establish bond of friendship and love between man and man.... It is necessary for us to understand the unique individuality of others, wherein lies the real language of the soul of man."[40] For establishing bond between education within four walls of classroom and society, Tagore gave stress on rural library services as he felt "a natural bond between education in the schools and colleges and the country outside them is immensely necessary."[41] For this he established mobile library '*Chalantika*' for the first time in India in 1925.[42]

Tagore's educational philosophy is postulated on three kinds of freedom, "freedom of mind," "freedom of heart," and "freedom of will." Tagore clarifies the concept of freedom "as God himself finds his own freedom in his own creation and then his nature is fulfiled, human beings have to create their own world and then they can have their freedom."[43] This freedom can be obtained only through space of mind. Tagore raised the question "What is space? It is freedom, not emptiness. Through this freedom of space child life finds its own voice...."[44] He expressed his "deep rooted convictions that only through freedom can man attain his fullness of growth."[45] The ever-expanding aspiration for fullness in man has two aspects which are interrelated; one, individual fullness; the other, social fullness. There is no gulf between the two. Library is the place which helps in expanding the horizon of all kinds of freedom through disseminating knowledge under its disposal.

As "whatever is worth knowing, is knowledge. It should be known equally by men and women—not for the sake of practical utility, but for the sake of knowing ...The desire to know is the law of human nature."[46] Tagore mentioned "we have come to this world, to accept it and not merely to know it. We may become powerful by knowledge, but we attain fullness by sympathy. The highest education is that which does not merely give us information but makes our life in harmony with all existence."[47] There is no nationality or caste in the field of knowledge. Man has a right to all the wealth created and produced by mankind....The knowledge that man has inherited is not the product of any single nation. The various streams of actions and knowledge of all mankind, flowing down through different ages, have merged together into the same ocean of the mind. Man is born on the stores of that intellectual ocean, whose call is sounded on all sides. Library as knowledge centre and integral part of present education system fulfils Tagorean vision of universe knowledge dissemination.

Conclusion

In five laws of library science Ranganathan gave stress on interaction between library and society. It is the responsibility of the society to provide books to all without loosing his/her time to get it. Not only that to keep the system of providing right document to right person at right time library must act like a "growing organism". Ranganathan in his Five laws gave special emphasis on the word 'every' that is right to knowledge by every citizen. Ranganathan thinks "...in libraries books are collected for USE, prepared for USE, kept for USE and served for USE."[48] For this reason library is a social and functional institution. Library is for the people, by the people and of the people. It should provide knowledge for development, prosperity of the society with freedom of joy to every individual's choice. Tagore expresses his vision of library in poetic language which is based on his educational philosophy. It demands active role of library by providing freedom of all kinds through disseminating knowledge and establishing bond with society as educational institutions are *"for them and by them"*.

References

1. Kaula, P.N. (1992), *An Autobiography of Dr. S.R. Ranganathan*. New Delhi: ABC Publishing House, p. 446.
2. Neelameghna, A., Library is a growing organism—S.R. Ranganathan. *DLIBCOM.* 2 (8-9) (2007): 2-3.
3. Ray, P.P. (2012), *Tagore in Print: A Comparative Study Before and After Expiry of Copyright*. New Delhi: Concept Publishing Company, p. 30.
4. Ray, P.P.; Biswas, B.C. and Sen, B.K. (2012): Vision of Library in Tagoreana: a study, *Srels Journal of Information Management*, 49(2) (2012): 145-154.

5. Tagore, Rabindranath (1929). Librarir mukhyo kartabyo. *The Indian Library Journal*. 2(2-4).
   (Speech prepared by Rabindranath Tagore, as the Chairman of Reception Committee of All India Libraries Association. Due to his illness it was read out by Mr. Hirendranath Dutta).
6. *Ibid.*
7. *Ibid.*
8. Tagore, Rabindranath. *Kshanika*. Calcutta: Visva-Bharati Granthan Vibhaga, 1359 (B.S.), p. 23.
9. Tagore, Rabindranath (1929). Librarir mukhyo kartabyo. *The Indian Library Journal*. 2(2-3).
10. Ranganathan, S.R. (1957) (rep. 1988), *The Five Laws of Library Science*. Bangalore: Sarada Ranganathan Endowment for Library Science, p. 33.
11. Tagore, Rabindranath. *Kanika*. Calcutta: Visva-Bharati Granthan Vibhaga, 1306 (B.S.), p. 5.
12. Tagore, Rabindranath. *Santiniketan Brahmacharyashrama*. Calcutta: Visva-Bharati Granthan Vibhaga, 1338 (B.S.), pp. 31-32.
13. Tagore, Rabindranath. *Katha sahitya*. Calcutta: Visva-Bharati Granthan Vibhaga, 1367(B.S.), p. 267.
14. Tagore, Rabindranath (1929). Librarir mukhyo kartabyo. *The Indian Library Journal*. 2(2-4).
15. *Ibid.*
16. Ranganathan, S.R. (1957) (rep.1988), *The Five Laws of Library Science*. Bangalore: Sarada Ranganathan Endowment for Library Science, p. 243.
17. Tagore, Rabindranath (1957). *Janmadine*. Calcutta: Visva-Bharati Granthan Vibhaga, p. 20.
18. Tagore, Rabindranath (1957). *Chhinapatravali*. Calcutta: Visva-Bharati Granthan Vibhaga, pp. 251-252.
19. Tagore, Rabindranath. *Jivansmriti*. Calcutta: Visva-Bharati Granthan Vibhaga, 1405 (B.S.), p. 13.
20. Tagore, Rabindranath. *Vithika*. Calcutta: Visva-Bharati Granthan Vibhaga, 1351 (B.S.), pp. 21-23.
21. Tagore, Rabindranath. *Chithipatra*, Vol. 5. Calcutta: Visva-Bharati Granthan Vibhaga, 1352 (B.S.), p. 139.
22. Tagore, Rabindranath. *Rabindra Rachanavali*, Vol. 4. Calcutta: Visva-Bharati Granthan Vibhaga, 1385 (B.S.), p. 559.
23. Tagore, Rabindranath. *Jivansmriti*. Calcutta: Visva-Bharati Granthan Vibhaga, 1405 (B.S.), pp. 70-71.
24. Tagore, Rabindranath. *Shiksha*. Calcutta: Visva-Bharati Granthan Vibhaga, 1342(B.S.), p. 87.
25. Bisi, Pramathanath. *Rabindranath o Santiniketan*. Calcutta: Visva-Bharati Granthan Vibhaga, 1402 (B.S.), p. 128.
26. Tagore, Rabindranath. *Punascha*. Calcutta: Visva-Bharati Granthan Vibhaga, 1372 (B.S.), pp. 13-14.

27. Tagore, Rabindranath (1951). *Naukadubi*. Calcutta: Visva-Bharati Granthan Vibhaga, p. 222.
28. Tagore, Rabindranath. *Siksar Herpher*. In *Siksha*. Calcutta: Visva-Bharati Granthan Vibhaga, 1412 (B.S.), p. 8.
29. Tagore, Rabindranath (1929). Librarir mukhyo kartabyo. *The Indian Library Journal*. 2(2-4).
30. *Ibid*.
31. *Ibid*.
32. Tagore, Rabindranath. *Letters from Russia*. Calcutta: Visva-Bharati Granthan Vibhaga, 1367 (B.S.), pp. 9-11.
33. Ranganathan, S.R. (1957) (rep.1988), *The Five Laws of Library Science*. Bangalore: Sarada Ranganathan Endowment for Library Science, p. 50.
34. Tagore, Rabindranath (1951). *My School*. In *Santiniketan: 1901-1951*. Calcutta: Visva-Bharati Granthan Vibhaga, pp. 6-7.
35. Ranganathan, S.R., (1957) (rep.1988), *The Five Laws of Library Science*. Bangalore: Sarada Ranganathan Endowment for Library Science, p. 327.
36. Tagore, Rabindranath. *Santiniketan Brahmacaryashrama*. Santiniketan: Visva-Bharati Granthan Vibhaga, 1358 (B.S.), p. 26.
37. Tagore, Rabindranath. *Santiniketan adiparba*. *Visva-Bharati Patrika*, Agrahayana 1349 (B.S.), p. 19.
38. Tagore, Rabindranath. *Shiksha*. Calcutta: Visva-Bharati Granthan Vibhaga, 1342 (B.S.), p. 260.
39. Tagore, Rabindranath. *Visva-Bharati*. Calcutta: Visva-Bharati Granthan Vibhaga, 1358 (B.S.), p. 122.
40. Tagore, Rabindranath. *Shiksha*. Calcutta: Visva-Bharati Granthan Vibhaga, 1342 (B.S.), p. 270.
41. Tagore, Rabindranath (1924). Schoolmaster. *Modern Review*. 36(3) (October 1924).
42. Ray, P.P. (2011). Public library service in Tagore's model of rural development: A study, In A Dasgupta (ed.) *LIS Profession in the Changing Environment*. Kolkata: IASLIC, pp. 161-174.
43. Tagore, Rabindranath (October 1924). *Schoolmaster*. *Modern Review*. Vol. 36(3).
44. Tagore, Rabindranath (1925). To the child. *Modern Review*. 37(2) (May).
45. Tagore, Rabindranath (1924). *Schoolmaster*. *Modern Review*, 36(3) (October).
46. Tagore, Rabindranath. *Shiksha*, Vol.1. Calcutta: Visva-Bharati Granthan Vibhaga, 1351 (B.S.), p. 181.
47. Tagore, Rabindranath (1970), *My School*. In *Lectures and Address*. Calcutta: MacMillan & Co., p. 21.
48. Ranganathan, S.R., (1957) (rep.1988), *The Five Laws of Library Science*. Bangalore: Sarada Ranganathan Endowment for Library Science, p. 68.

2

Influence of Manu on Ranganathan's Philosophy of Library Science

An Overview

Introduction

Shiyali Ramamrita Ranganathan (1892-1972) is known to the world for this contribution for the establishment and advancement of Library Science and also library profession. No profession can be established without a solid theoretical, philosophical foundation and its practical implementation. Ranganathan not only gave philosophical foundation to library science as social science, but also its practical implication in library towards fulfilment of its social goal through his numerous laws, theories, principles and canons. Now, the question is what are the influencing factors behind the philosophy of Ranganathan? Ranganathan had great interest in Sanskrit literature from his early ages. In his matured writings numerous quotations from Sanskrit literature can be traced.

Manu has narrated Hindu code of conduct and ways of obeying the code of law known as *Manu Samhita* or *Manusmriti* ("Laws of Manu"). This *Manava-Dharmashastra* consists of two thousand six hundred and ninety four *Sutras* in twelve chapters. It narrates proclaim duties of people at various stages of life, dietary regulation rights and duties of rulers etc. Thus, *Manu Samhita* has tremendous impact on society as "the law of all the social classes" as even recognized by the *Vedas*. "Manu became the lawgiver par excellence, and his name, a byword for what was righteous proper. The *Vedas* say whatever Manu said is wholesome like medicine, *Yad vai kinchana Manur avadad tad bheshajam*." "In usages it covers a wide range of meaning from the qualities and characteristics of the things to the highest virtue and spiritual efforts; natural characteristics and tendencies, as also what men should do or ought to do."[1]

Manu's Influence on Ranganathan

Manu Samhita covers all aspects of four stages (*Ashramas*) of life—*Brahmacharya* (the student age), *Grihastha* (the householder age), *Vanaprastha* (the hermit stage) and *Sannyasa* (the wandering ascetic stage). Second and third chapter of *Manu Samhita* narrated *Brahmacharya*—which deals with students' duty during learning process and also teacher's (*Acharya*) role in the teaching-learning process. Library as knowledge hub tries to fulfil the objectives as well as spread of education. Library as knowledge centre collects, stores, organises and disseminates knowledge to meet individual as well as social thrust of knowledge. In dealing with the users librarian also follows some professional ethics or code of conduct while discharging their duties. A librarian's behaviour is same like a teacher to his new student. He has to be hospitable just like a host. According to Manu "Grass, room (for resting), water, and fourthly a kind word; these (things) never fail in the houses of a good man."[2] In the same tone Ranganathan opinioned " …a library, keen about its books being fully used, will plant itself in the midst of its clientele."[3] "Library alone can be called hospitable, which shows an eagerness to invite readers to the feast at its disposal, it is such hospitability that makes a library big not in size."[4]

Ranganathan read *Manu Samhita* and influenced by its code relating to conduct of student-teacher. As he correctly mentioned that librarian has to attempt all efforts to satisfy its users like teachers to his student. "Sometimes, all conscious attempts fail. Hence, we have to act on the principle of the more, the merrier. By contacting the student intimately in varied situation, we may increase the chance to hit their nuclear element. So, little is ever achieved by verbal transmission. A true teacher fulfils himself more effectively through that intangible influence emanating from his personality and transforms the students and throws them into the most favourable mood for the creative enfoldment of their own personality."[5] One may think that Ranganathan's opinion originates from Manu's narration, "The good should be taught to people without hurting them; one who desires merit should use his words sweetly and delicately."[6]

In ancient education system a student has to pass through the code of ordinances of studentship which includes subduing the senses, rules of study, respectful social dealing with fellow citizen, stages of rituals as well as behavioural pattern so that they might become good citizen. It was expected that later on the student will became teacher and follow the same tradition to teach his pupils. According to Manu among four stages of life *Brahmacharya* be considered as best as it forms the foundation of other stages of life. This stage helps to develop knowledge base of individual as well as of the society. Prof. Raghavan has rightly mentioned " ...the term *Brahmacharya* means also celibacy and continence."[7] According to Manu "...the knowledge of the soul is state to be the most excellent among all of them; for that is the first of all sciences, because immortality is gained through that."[8] One can notice same kind of observation from Ranganathan's classic work "School library: the training ground for responsible citizenship." It highlights as training ground "it (library) promotes: (1) Public mindedness; (2) Consideration for others: (2.1) Right attitude towards obligation of public life; (2.2) Avoidance of difficulties to the other members of the community; (3) Respect for the rule of the queue; (4) Formation of correct habits of public and private hygiene; (5) Fire Prevention; and (6) Personal manners."[9] To comply these right attitudes is essential. Now, the question may rise what attitude ought to be considered as right? To Answer this question again one have to turn to Manu "Learn that sacred law which is followed by men learned (in the *Veda*) and assented to in their hearts by the virtuous, who are ever exempt from hatred and inordinate affection."[10] Again as a genesis of Ranganathan's concept of "Avoidance of difficulties..." one may consider *Manu Samhita* as source "Let him not, even though in pain, (speak words) cutting (others) to the quick, let him not injure others in thought or deed; let him not utter speeches which make (others) afraid of him, since that will prevent him from gaining heaven."[11] Respect for the rule of the law in "Personal manners" may find its genesis from Manu, "The rule of conduct is transcendent law, whether it be taught in the revealed texts or in the sacred tradition; hence a twice born man who possesses regard for himself, should be always careful to (follow) it."[12]

Many times while providing services to the users in library it may not be possible to satisfy them to utmost level. As an ongoing process library has to take feedback from user to develop or modify search strategy. Ranganathan in "Prolegomena to Library

Classification" mentioned "When one is engaged on a problem, the most useful ideas occur suddenly. They seem at once to cast a flood of light over murky tracts of half-formed thought and promise reward to further exploration..."[13] For philosophical genesis of this statement one can look upon Manu "Let him not despise himself on account of former failure; until death let him seek fortune, not despair of gaining it."[14]

Five Laws of Library Science

Ranganathan has used twice (once after the contents and again in description of Second Law under "Manu's Maxim") the following quotations of *Manu Samhita* in his classic work "The Five Laws of Library Science."

> **यो दद्याज्ज्ञानमज्ञानां कुर्याद्वा धर्मदर्शनम्।**
> **स कृत्स्नां पृथिवीं दद्यात् तेन तुल्यं न तद्भवेत्।।** **मनुः।**

Which means:

> "To carry knowledge to the door of those that lack it and to educate all to perceive the right!
> Even to give away the whole earth cannot equal that form of service."[15]

Influence of Manu can easily be understood when Ranganathan devoted a paragraph on "Manu's Maxim" in "second law and its *digvijaya*" for the sake of spread of education. He mentioned "We cannot end this rapid sketch of the World Conquering Expedition of the Second Law of Library Science more appropriately than by praying, in all sincerity, for the speedy success of the Second Law in India as well and by reminding our Ministers of Education that the example of their brethren in the progressive nations is but in close consonance with the precept of our ancient law-giver."[16]

Ranganathan in his Five Laws gave special emphasis on the word 'every' that is the right to knowledge by every citizen. As "... in library books are collected for Use, prepared for Use, kept for Use and served for Use."[17] It may again be derived from the Manu's narration of man without book, with book, knowledgeable man after study and chance of his behaviour thereafter. To quote Manu "(Even forgetful) student of the (sacred) books are more distinguished than the ignorant, those who remember them surpass the (forgetful) students, those who possess a knowledge (of the meaning) are more distinguished than those who (only) remember (the words), men who follow (the teaching of the texts) surpass those who (merely) know (their meaning)."[18] The same concept has been reflected in Ranganathan's Five Laws—"When knower and knowee are brought into relation, the knower knows the knowee; and knowledge emerges."[19]

For maximum use of library service the role, relationship, behaviour, attitude of librarian is most important. Ranganathan in First Law under the heading "What makes a Library Big" mentioned "In fact, the relationship between the librarian and the reader should be easiest and the most agreeable….."[20] ".. it is the Library Staff that ultimately makes or mars a library."[21] The same kind of atmosphere one can notice in family life "…where the husband is pleased with the wife and the wife with her husband, happiness will assuredly lasting."[22]

Discussion

Ranganathan was greatly influenced by Indian epic. One can find ample examples in his numerous writings. Such as in narration of First law he mentioned Lord Krishna's words of *Karmayoga* to the librarians:

> "Thy right is to action alone and never to fruits.
> Let not the fruit of action be the motive.
> Nor let thyself be attached to inaction."[23]

Again in Vital Principle to make it understand "the spirit of the library" as knowledge centre he took help from *Gita*:

> "As a person casts off worn-out garments and puts on others that are new, so does the embodied soul cast off worn-out forms and enter into others that are new.
>
> Weapons do not cleave him; fire does not burn him; water does not make him wet; nor does the wind make him dry.
>
> He cannot be cloven; he cannot be burnt; he cannot be wetted; he cannot be dried; he is eternal, all-pervading, steadfast and immovable; he is the same for ever."[24]

Thus in many occasions to narrate, collaborate or substantiate Ranganathan used Indian Mythology and *Manu Samhita* is of no exception. "If *Manusmrti* is not a mere code of ordinate duties, and if it raises in its philosophical parts to grave dignity, it ranks high also as a masterpiece of ancient literature which is pithy and effective couplets gives expression to some of the most precious ideas and noblest virtues and ideals."[25] Moreover, *Manu Samhita* also known as *Manava-Dharmashastra* has a great impact on society. Likewise "Library is a social and functional organization." So, Manu's impact in respect of philosophical aspects on library is obvious. Particularly, when it describes *Brahmacharya*—the main focus is on creating knowledge society in a disciplined way. To strive for knowledge is to struggle for freedom as ignorance is the worst slavery. "As an elephant made of wood, as an antelope made of leather, such is an unlearned Brahmana; those there have nothing but the names (of their kind)."[26]

Conclusion

Concept of knowledge based society can be traced from ancient Indian education system through oral tradition of disseminating knowledge called *Shruti. Manu Samhita* by providing guiding principle had laid the foundation of knowledge based society. Ranganathan being influenced by Indian mythology in general and *Manu Samhita* in particular foster the way by providing all kinds of philosophical as well as functional aspects of library as store house and disseminator of recorded knowledge. Only through equal access to education, information, knowledge to every citizen knowledge society can be established where freedom of expression will persist. Then only freedom of mind, freedom of heart and freedom of will be established.

"Ranganathan's *'Five Laws of Library Science'*, propounded succinctly each in four to six words only, is the epitome of the operational philosophy of librarianship."[27] This is because Five Laws are based on solid philosophical foundation based on Indian *Dharmashastra* can be extended to any limit and contemporary. Laws may be interpreted in different ways, but the spirit remains the same. Gorman interpreted Ranganathan's Laws in the context of today's libraries and its possible futures known as Gorman's Five New Laws of Librarianship.[28] Again it is possible to replace Books by Links, Software, Information, Knowledge, Tapes, Files,

Records etc. Further, it may even be extended to different organizations like museums, class rooms, groceries, patients, temple considering these laws as common laws as proposed by Prof. B.K. Sen.[29]

References

1. Raghavan, V., 1962, *The Manu Samhita*. In *The Cultural Heritage of India*, vol. 2. Ed. S.K. De, *et al.*, Calcutta: Ramakrishna Mission Institute of Culture, p. 335.
2. Buhlar, G., 1988, *The Laws of Manu: Translated with Extracts from Seven Commentaries. Sacred Books of the East Series*, vol. 25. Ed. Max Muller. Delhi: Motilal Banarasidass, p. 93.
3. Ranganathan, S.R., 1957 (rep.1988), *The Five Laws of Library Science*. Bangalore: Sarada Ranganathan Endowment for Library Science, p. 33.
4. Tagore, R., 1929, Librarir mukhyo kartabyo. *The Indian Library Journal*. 2(2-3).
5. Ranganathan, S.R., 1966, *New Education and School Library: Experience of Half a Century*. Bangalore: Sarada Ranganathan Endowment for Library Science, (rep.), p. 73.
6. Raghavan, V., 1962, *The Manu Samhita*. In *The Cultural Heritage of India*, vol. 2. Ed. S.K. De, *et al.*, Calcutta: Ramakrishna Mission Institute of Culture, p. 357.
7. *Ibid.*, p. 346.
8. Buhlar, G., 1988, *The Laws of Manu: Translated with Extracts from Seven Commentaries. Sacred Books of the East Series*, vol. 25. Ed. Max Muller. Delhi: Motilal Banarasidass, p. 501.
9. Ranganathan, S.R., 1966, *New Education and School Library: Experience of Half a Century*. Bangalore: Sarada Ranganathan Endowment for Library Science, (rep.), p. 228.
10. Buhlar, G., 1988, *The Laws of Manu: Translated with Extracts from Seven Commentaries. Sacred Books of the East Series*, vol. 25. Ed. Max Muller. Delhi: Motilal Banarasidass, p. 29.
11. *Ibid.*, p. 28.
12. *Ibid.*, p. 27.
13. Ranganathan, S.R., 1989, *Prolegomena to Library Classification*. Bangalore: Sarada Ranganathan Endowment for Library Science, p. 21.
14. Buhlar, G., 1988, *The Laws of Manu: Translated with Extracts from Seven Commentaries. Sacred Books of the East Series*, vol. 25. Ed. Max Muller. Delhi: Motilal Banarasidass, p. 150.
15. Ranganathan, S.R., 1957 (rep.1988), *The Five Laws of Library Science*.

Bangalore: Sarada Ranganathan Endowment for Library Science, p. 9.
16. *Ibid.*, p. 189.
17. *Ibid.*, p. 68.
18. Buhlar, G., 1988, *The Laws of Manu: Translated with Extracts from Seven Commentaries. Sacred Books of the East Series,* vol. 25. Ed. Max Muller. Delhi: Motilal Banarasidass, pp. 507-508.
19. Ranganathan, S.R., 1957 (rep.1988), *The Five Laws of Library Science.* Bangalore: Sarada Ranganathan Endowment for Library Science, p. 358.
20. *Ibid.*, p. 77.
21. *Ibid.*, p. 50.
22. Buhlar, G., 1988, *The Laws of Manu: Translated with Extracts from Seven Commentaries. Sacred Books of the East Series,* vol. 25. Ed. Max Muller. Delhi: Motilal Banarasidass, p. 86.
23. Ranganathan, S.R., 1957 (rep.1988), *The Five Laws of Library Science.* Bangalore: Sarada Ranganathan Endowment for Library Science, p. 79.
24. *Ibid.*, p. 354.
25. Raghavan, V., 1962, *The Manu Samhita.* In *The Cultural Heritage of India,* vol. 2. Ed. S.K. De, *et al.*, Calcutta: Ramakrishna Mission Institute of Culture, p. 357.
26. Buhlar, G., 1988, *The Laws of Manu: Translated with Extracts from Seven Commentaries. Sacred Books of the East Series,* vol. 25. Ed. Max Muller. Delhi: Motilal Banarasidass, p. 59.
27. Mukherjee, A.K., 1966, *Librarianship its Philosophy and History.* Bombay: Asia Publishing House, p. 31.
28. Gorman, M., Five New Laws of Librarianship. *American Libraries.* 26(8)(1995).
29. Sen, B.K., 2008, Ranganathan's Five Laws. *Annals of Library and Information Studies,* 55 (June): 87-90.

3

Information for Tribal Development

A Case Study of Santal's Attitude and Adjustment

Introduction

Information is considered as one of the most powerful instrument for sustainable socio-economic development. It is expected that educated people will generate and consume more information. Only through education human society can develop their knowledge-base by gathering information on every aspect of life. Recognizing this aspect Constitution of India in its Article 45 (Directive Principles of State Policies) states, "The State shall endeavour to provide, within a period of ten years from commencement of this Constitution, for free and compulsory education for all children until the complete the age of fourteen years." Special emphasis has been given for educational development of the weaker section in Article 46, which narrates "The State shall promote with special care the educational and economic interest of the weaker sections of the people, and in particular, of the Schedules Castes and Scheduled Tribes."[1] To fulfil this goal Government and NGOs have adopted multifarious measures for educational development of the people, especially people belonging to Scheduled Caste (SC) and Scheduled Tribe (ST) communities, to make them aware about need for information, knowledge for development. Initiatives like *Sarva Shiksha Abhiyan, Right to Information Act, National Knowledge Commission* recommendation are some of the recent efforts in this direction. But the development process would be successful if (i) the beneficiaries become increasable aware of themselves and the world they live in, and specially of their capacity to transform it; and (ii) the recipients are helped to remove obstacles to personal growth.[2]

Significance of the Study

Education is considered as an indispensable "passport to life" not only to enable to people to choose their occupation, but also to eradicate the inequalities between different groups and sexes. In India during the last five decades several strategies and approaches for tribal development were adopted. The sub-plan area approach has adopted since the Fifth Five Year Plan, has classified tribal areas into three broad categories, i.e. (i) tribal concentrated areas, (ii) tribal dispersed areas, and (iii) primitive tribal pockets. The sub-plan area approach is aimed at integrating various developmental activities besides flexibility in planning and resource allocation.[3]

But even after seventy years of Independence it is observed that in spite of both Governmental and Non-governmental efforts on tribal development, progress in the tribal development in respect of rate of literacy, per capita income, consumption etc. is not up to the mark. Rate of literacy among the tribal people in our country is very disappointing. It reveals that various endeavours to spread education among tribes have failed to convince most of the tribal people.[4] Even if they are realizing the need for education information, they are not able to adopt it properly. Maybe they are still in so much steeped in stigma and taboos that they fail to perceive the significance of information in one life for individual as well as social development. But, in spite of these premonitions a flicker of hope is visible. As we can observe increase rate of literacy of tribal people from various census reports, increase in per capita income, consumption as well as access to various information sources formal and non-formal. Perhaps due to the impact of mass media and other programmes, different projects and programmes launched by the government and NGOs, some changes might have occurred in the attitude and adjustment capacity of the younger folks of the tribal society. Some positive influence of rich socio-cultural and educational environment nearby cannot also be ruled out in this regard.

Whatever be the case it seems imperative that an objective survey is done to investigate into the attitude of the tribal people towards information as an instrument for development and also their capacity to adjust in the changing environment to find out, if there has been any change in their attitude in so many years after

Independence. Such a study is very much needed for deciding our next course of action for removing ignorance and illiteracy from tribal people. This study is expected to contribute significantly in the field of library and information science by throwing light on some unexplored areas of role of information and its communication for development.

Objectives of the Study

- To find out the attitude of the first generation, second generation and third generation of tribal people in the four Santal villages towards information.
- To find out the difference in attitude, if any, between the first generation and second generation, second generation and third generation and between first generation and third generation towards information.
- To find out significant change of attitude (if any) towards information has occurred across the generations.

Hypothesis

Following hypothesis is drawn on the basis of assumption that attitudes are modifiable and attitudes of the respondents are reflected in the attitude scale prepared for this purpose:

H_1: The attitude of Santal tribes belonging to second generation differs from that of Santals of first generation.

H_2: The attitude of the Santal belonging to third generation differs from that of Santals of second generation.

H_3: The attitude of the Santal belonging to third generation towards information differs from that of Santals of first generation.

Population of the Study

There are 11 tribal races in the district of Birbhum of West Bengal comprising 7 per cent of total population of the district. The Santals are distributed in 7 Gram Panchayats (GPs) of the district Birbhum.[5] The study was made over 20 households comprising 60 individuals of 4 villages (Kaliganj, Chakpali, Koyetpukur and Sarpukurdanga) of 3 GPs, namely Ruppur, Stator and Kasba. Three GPs are within the radius of (± 4-8 km) from Santiniketan, the international famous educational/cultural central university of national importance and the villages are at 5-10 km distance from sub-divisional town of Birbhum district, Bolpur.

Table 3.1: Santal Population Distributed in Households

Sl. No.	*Literacy*	*GP*	*Village*	*No. of Households*		*Population*	*Rate of*	
				M	*F*	*Total*	*M*	*F*
1.	Ruppur	Kaliganj	70	190	193	383	67.90	35.23
		Chakpali	20	44	43	87	74.80	27.90
2.	Stator	Koyetpukur	41	94	87	181	42.55	24.14
3.	Kasba	Sarpukurdanga	38	94	88	182	57.47	30.68

Source: Survey by the Author.

Methodology and Tools Used

For measuring the attitude of the tribal women towards information, two attitude scales of Likert[6] type had been administered. As survey was conducted on three successive generations, two attitude scales were constructed—one for the adult tribal people (belonging to first and second generation, Appendix-B) and another for young tribal people belonging to third generation (*Vide* Appendix-A).

Analysis and Interpretation of Data

After collecting data from 60 respondents (20 from each generation) the investigator scored each response sheets individually. After computing the total attitude score of each respondent individually the mean attitude score of each of the group was computed. Then the investigator tried to find out whether the mean difference between any two groups was significant or not. Three formulated hypothesis were verified in the following manner:

> H_1: The attitude of Santal belonging to second generation differs from that of the first generation (*see* Table 3.2).

The result reveals that the attitude of the Santals belonging to the second generation does not differ significantly from that of Santals of first generation. So, H_1 is rejected. Difference is being found between two mean attitudes scores is due to sampling fluctuation.

Table 3.2: Difference of mean attitude score of 1st and 2nd generation of Santal Tribe

Sample	*Mean (M)*	*D (D = M_1- M_2)*	*D*	*t (t = D/ D)*	*df df = (N – 1) + (N – 1) where N = 20*	*Level of significance (L.S)*
First Geneneration Second Generation	71.8 (M_1) 73.95 (M_2)	2.15	1.65	1.30	38	0.05
Result	$t_{cal} < t_{tab}$ at 0.05 L.S. Since the value is insignificant, therefore, H_1 is rejected.					

H_2 : The attitude of the Santals belonging to third generation differs from that of Santals of second generation.

Table 3.3: Difference of mean attitude score of 2nd and 3rd generation of Santal Tribe

Mean (M)	*Score*	*t*	*Accepted level of Significance 0.05*
Second Generation (M_2)	73.95	—	—
Third Generation (M_3)	70.5	1.71	N.S.

The above result reveals that H_2 is rejected as the obtained value is 1.71 which does not reach t = –2.02 at 0.05 level. It follows that obtained difference between the mean attitude score of the second and third generation is not significant. That means the attitude of the Santals belonging to the third generation is not different from that of the Santals of second generation.

H_3: The attitude of the Santals belonging to the third generation towards education differs from that of the first generation.

Table 3.4: Difference of mean attitude score of 1st and 3rd generation of Santal Tribe

Mean (M)	*Score*	*t*	*Accepted level of Significance 0.05*
First Generation (M_1)	71.8	—	—
Third Generation (M_3)	70.5	0.62	N.S.

The result reveals that the attitude of the Santals belonging to first generation does not differ significantly from that of the Santals of third generation. Hence, H_3 is rejected. The difference of mean attitude score is due to sampling fluctuation.

In order to know the number of Santals having decidedly favourable attitude towards information, the collected data were organized in a different way. M – .50 was taken as cut off point for determining decidedly favourable attitude towards information. The mean-att-score and S.D. of 60 respondents were calculated.

M was found to be 72.08 and S.D. = 6.03
72.03 + 3.01
or 72 + 3 = 75.

75 was considered to be the cut off point in this study, which means that Santals having scores above 75 would be regarded as those having decidedly favourable attitude towards information. The findings are as follows:

Table 3.5: Generation-wise favourable attitude towards information

Generation	*No. of subject considered in the study*	*No.of Santals having Decidedly favourable attitude*	*% of Santals having decidedly favourable attitude*
First	20	7	35
Second	20	12	60
Third	20	9	45

Taking all consideration, M –.50 was considered as cut off point for deciding unfavourable attitude towards information. As mentioned earlier, mean attitude score of 60 respondent is 72.08, SD = 6.03.

M – .50 = 72 – 3 = 69.

Therefore, 69 is taken as the cut off point in this study which means that Santals having score below 69 would be regarded as those having decidedly unfavourable attitude towards information. The findings are shown in Table 3.6.

A generation-wise change of Santal having decidedly favourable/unfavourable attitude towards information can be observed from Tables 3.5 and 3.6.

Table 3.6: Generation-wise unfavourable attitude towards information

Generation	No. of subjects considered in the study	No. of Santals having decidedly unfavourable attitude towards information	% of Santals having decidedly unfavourable attitude towards information
First	20	5	25
Second	20	3	15
Third	20	6	30

Discussion

Above tables (3.2–3.4) indicates that inter-generation significance of difference in attitude towards information, does not significantly differ among the first and second generation, second and third generation and first and third generation of the Santals. Minor difference observed in these respect may be described as sampling fluctuation.

But, Tables 3 .5 and 3.6 reveal a different picture. Though the results of 't' test was non-significant at all three age groups, i.e. between first and second, second and third, first and third generation. These Tables show that:

(a) Largest percentage (60%) of Santals showing decidedly favourable attitude towards information belongs to the second generation.
(b) Simultaneously decidedly unfavourable attitude towards information is also lowest (15%) among the women belonging to second generation (Table 3.6).

Apart from this statistical data it was observed during informal discussion with the Santals (second generation) that at present adult Santals have strong inclination towards information in general and education in particular. They expressed their opinion that their parents could not realize the importance of education; they could not be educated and were obliged to continue the occupation as their parents. But, now they do not want to repeat the mistake of their parents and want their children (third generation) to be informed and educated so that they could opt for any occupation suitable for them. They want their children (irrespective of sex) to be informed and educated. They think if their daughters are educated they could find a suitable match for them and /or a good job. They also think only well informed people would understand things in their right perspective. This will not only improve their life style but also make them better human being too, which they think very important for their life. The investigator also observed that the more they are thinking of all these aspects the more they are convinced about the advantages of getting more information. And most striking thing is that even at this age they themselves are prepared to attend informal schools and study even after whole-days' hard work.

It was also observed that there are Santal parents who want their children to attend schools and feel the urge of it—but in actual practice fail to send them to school as helping hands are required for collecting fuel, fetching water, cooking and looking after young ones, while they are away at work. At times the economic condition of the family compels the children to contribute to the family wage basket prematurely.

Though from statistical analysis the attitude towards information between the first generation Santals and the third generation Santals did not differ significantly, yet informal discussion with the first generation revealed that their attitude is something different from the attitude of the third generation. Elderly Santals now feel that their inefficiency, incapability in getting, understanding, analysing information an associated problems, they are facing in their day-to-day life are due to lack of education. It is true for the Santal second generation also. If adequate teaching, library and other formal and informal information channels are provided that would suit their convenience they will definitely participate in such venture along with their children. Maybe they have fully realized that information is now power to improve quality of life.

On the contrary the young learners (10–15) possess an entirely different attitude towards information. This group showed highest percentage of having decidedly unfavourable attitude towards information (*vide* Table 3.5) while their mothers hold remarkably favourable attitude towards information. The investigator feels that such a retrogressive movement of attitude towards information needs an in-depth probes. However, this unusual phenomenon may be explained in the following manner:

(a) In our existing system of school, regular attendance is obligatory for any student. But, the researcher through his formal discussion with young learner and also through his own observation felt that the obligation of school discipline or other information dissemination centre is not in tune with the liberty and freedom normally a tribal child is accustomed with. They like moving together, sing, dance and gossip at will and /or fishing small fish, rats or birds etc. So, they got bored in the formal present day education system.

(b) During the 'try-out' phase of the instrument for their study and also during the present survey a few respondents expressed that they want to go to traditional information dissemination centres as their parents want to go them. This may be because it is an inherent nature of the Santals that they are concerned with the 'present' not with 'future development'. Hence, they fail to understand the importance of long-range benefit of information.

(c) Santals enjoyed the other way of life more attractive because it is full of fun. Whereas a prolonged formal process of becoming knowledgeable deter them from all these readily available pleasure.

(d) It was noticed during investigation that though most of the Santals residing in and around Santiniketan is bi-lingual, yet the medium of information communication (Bengali) poses some problem for them.

Conclusion

The Santals of the population under study have an active exposure to poly-ethnic association, and are living with other speech community people within a diverse geo-cultural frame. Santals have their own traditional information communication system. But, now they are using modern communication techniques available in the area to articulate and adjust with the contemporary situation and non-Santals. They have village council and council executives who are still functioning in different rites and rituals of the Santals, and acts as communication agents. The traditional form of communication like myths and legends; songs and dance, fairs and festivals have an active role in the life of culture as well as socio-economic development that has propagated through generations.

Thus, if we consider communication agents—two types of information communication agents are working in the society—traditional and modern. A balance between the two forms of information communication has to be drawn for proper information communication for development and it is necessary for cultural adjustment as well as change of attitude in time.

The possible strategy for information communication in tribal areas may be:

(i) Creation of information products or secondary sources relating to information needed by rural people for their development. The information products may be required in the areas of healthcare, social welfare, education, agriculture, animal husbandry, cottage industries, finance and investment. If possible the information may be provided in local language with emphasis on local culture.

(ii) Establishment of Information Dissemination Centres: Public library system has to be developed and strengthened to act as community information centres. Resources of different agencies engaged in the field of public health, adult education, local self-government and such others may be pooled to build up the resource base of these libraries. A proper co-ordination and communication in different government departments to ensure flow of right information at right time to right people for development is must. Establishment of information kiosks may be the right direction in this respect. Information is power. NGOs have great opportunity to work in this area. The ultimate aim of all these efforts should be to bring this power to the poor rural masses and make them conscious about the strength of information, in a word to develop information culture.

References

1. Basu, D.D., (1998) *Shorter Constitution of India*. New Dehi: Prentice Hall of India, p. 69.
2. Deogaonkar, G.G. (1994), *Tribal Administration and Development*. New Delhi: Concept Publishing Company, p. 98.
3. Murti, K.S. and Rao, K.V. (2004), Primary education of tribes in backward region in Andhra Pradesh: A Case study. In *Census 2001 & Human Development in India,* Ramachandrudu, D.Ed. New Delhi: Serials Publications, p. 190.
4. Rath, G.C. (2006), *Tribal Development in India: The Contemporary Debate*. New Delhi: Sage Publications.
5. *Census of India 2001. Available (Online) <censusindia.gov.in>,* visited on 12.12.2015.
6. Likert, R. (1982), *A Technique for the Measurement of Attitude*. New York: The Science Press, p. 140.

APPENDIX-A

Attitude Scale Towards Information for Santal Children

Put a tick mark in the respective columns against the statement.

Sl. No.	*Statements*	*Support the Statement*	*Neutral about the Statement*	*Oppose the Statement*
1.	People became fool if they are not well informed.			
2.	To be well informed is beyond our reach, so, it is better not to be informed.			
3.	I am very eager to be informed.			
4.	We can learn many things through information.			
5.	Other children do not go to formal educational institution, then why should I?			
6.	It is better not to be informed.			
7.	To be established in life information and education are essential.			
8.	Pupil belonging to other community does not mix with us in the institution where formal education is provided.			
9.	We can learn many things from school and I like to go there.			
10.	Information will not help us to lead better life; we are in the same condition like before.			
11.	Information can help us to understand what is happening in and around us.			

(*Contd.*)

Sl. No.	*Statements*	*Support the Statement*	*Neutral about the Statement*	*Oppose the Statement*
12.	Education what we get from school or other institution does not help us to lead our daily life.			
13.	Information helps us to take proper decision.			
14.	If we go to formal educational institution, we shall not get time to gossip with our friends.			
15.	We can take decision about signing on a paper if we are informed about the content of it.			
16.	We have to work at home or others house, so what we shall do by being well informed.			
17.	If we became informed, educated we can read and understand things better.			
18.	After hard work all through the day, we do not like all these ideas.			
19.	We can seek some other job except daily labour if we are educated, and trained.			
20.	Parents tell us about all these things (education, information, knowledge etc.), but I do not like it.			
21.	We receive information in Bengali, English language which is foreign to us and difficult to understand.			

(Contd.)

Sl. No.	*Statements*	*Support the Statement*	*Neutral about the Statement*	*Oppose the Statement*
22.	Information can help us to get all kinds of benefits provided by the Government.			
23.	We cannot memorise things even after repeated practice, so we became disinterested about it.			
24.	If we are well informed nobody can ditch us.			
25.	Education has no need in our life we are satisfied with the present state of affairs.			
26.	We enjoy things better what is happening around us when we can analysis it on the basis of our knowledge/information.			

APPENDIX-B

Attitude scale towards Information for Santal Parents

Put a tick mark in the respective columns against the statement

Sl. No.	*Statements*	*Support the Statement*	*Neutral about the Statement*	*Oppose the Statement*
1.	People became fool if they are not well-informed.			
2.	Informed children will not obey their parents.			
3.	It is essential to be informed, to lead a good life.			
4.	We receive information in Bengali, English language which is foreign to us and difficult to understand.			

(Contd.)

Sl. No.	*Statements*	*Support the Statement*	*Neutral about the Statement*	*Oppose the Statement*
5.	Information can help us to get all kinds of benefits provided by the Government.			
6.	Pupil belonging to other community does not mix with us in the formal educational institutions.			
7.	Informed educated children want to enjoy luxury life spending more money, so it is better to avoid it.			
8.	If we are well informed nobody can ditch us.			
9.	It is better to purchase food, then spent money for education.			
10.	It is easy to arrange marriage with employed bride if children are educated.			
11.	Children do much work at home, so, we are not interested to send them to school.			
12.	If we became informed, educated we can read and understand things better.			
13.	If women became educated, they can teach the children.			
14.	It becomes difficult to arrange marriage, if the girls become educated, informed as they will select their bride according to their choice.			
15.	We can take decision about signing on a paper if we are informed about the content of it.			
16.	To be well informed is beyond our reach, so, it is better not to be informed.			

(Contd.)

Sl. No.	*Statements*	*Support the Statement*	*Neutral about the Statement*	*Oppose the Statement*
17.	We can learn many new things through information.			
18.	Information will help us to get proper wages for our labour.			
19.	We could have been educated if we get facility like present generation.			
20.	Education has no need in our life we are satisfied with the present state of affairs.			
21.	We can enjoy if we can communicate things in our own handwritings.			
22.	Nobody in our generation is well informed, so we can receive no benefit with huge information.			
23.	We can gather information if information centres are available in our close proximity.			
24.	It is not possible for us to engage our children in formal institution during harvesting season			
25.	Informed and educated generation is being detached from our society.			
26.	We can avail facility from Panchayat, Post Office, bank etc. if we are informed educated.			

4

Matrimonial (Socio-Economic) Choice and Bradford's Law

A Study

Introduction

Human beings are social animals that live in a society. "Society is a system of usages and procedures, of authority and mutual aid, of many grouping and divisions, of controls of human behaviour and of liberties. This ever-changing, complex system we call society. It is the web of social relationships. And it is ever changing."[1] Families are considered as core and care institutions across culture that helps in formation and transformation of society. Their essential function, historically, has been to contribute to the basic economic survival of family members; thus, the structure of families often adapts to the economy, and cultural ideologies and laws are created to reinforce that adaptation. "By structure of the family is meant its formal patterning of rights, duties and living arrangements and its defined status of age, sex and kingship."[2] "A joint family is a group of people who generally live under one roof, who eat food cooked at one hearth, who hold property in common and who participate in common family worship and are related to each other as some particular type of kindred."[3] Factors like characteristics of authority and common income, property, mutual rights and obligations are also part of it. The joint family is being converted to isolated nuclear family due to industrialization and urbanization. Urbanization based on economy and technological development makes a revolutionary change in the whole pattern of social life.

Marriage has almost universally been defined as a social and legal union between men and women, although a few cultures have allowed people of the same sex to marry.[4] The sociologist Max Weber defined marriage as a "stable sexual relationship" allowed and legitimized by the larger kin group and used to determine rules about property rights for children. The majority of marriages are based on monogamy, i. e. a union between single man and single woman, but other kinds of marriages such as polygamous marriages also exist. Knowledge about caste system in India is necessary to understand family life. The numerous castes and sub-castes are arranged in a series of chain and array of castes so that each caste members knows his super ordinate, subordinate and coordinate position. "Thus, the whole caste system is a very intricate structure which places social groups on innumerable and minute steps indicative of status and function."[5]

India is a country of unity among diversity. In social sphere also there is diversity in respect of race, ethnicity, culture, language, religion, customs etc. Difference in socio-economic status, education, social choice, power, gender biasness etc. can also be noticed. Many of these play key role for selecting a marriage partner. Social marriage is considered as not only a marriage between two, but two families. So, smooth flow of all socio-economic-cultural information is necessary for matrimonial purpose. A good number of sources right from human sources (like *Ghatak, Kul-purohit*) to print media to electronic media is available. A daily or weekly newspaper with matrimonial classified information (with information about bride or bridegroom with all communication information) plays a key role for disseminating information.

In a marriage socio-economic choice plays a predominant role in selection of bride and bridegroom. The choices are many and vary from person to person. But there may be some core choice. "Bradford's law of scattering"[6] was applied to identify and test whether there are core choices. A good number of papers on different theoretical aspects of Bradford law had been published.[7-13] The law had been applied for literature review[14-18], bibliography[19-21], library acquisition[22-24], citation analysis[25-28], in different discipline[29] even to identify core personality[30] in personal communication.

Objectives of the Study

- To identify core socio-economic choice during marriage of bride and bridegrooms;

- To identify difference in core choice of bride and bridge grooms; and
- To find out whether matrimonial (socio-economic) choice follow Bradford's law.

Methodology

The basic data for this study was collected from two leading Bengali dailies, namely *Anandabazar Patrika* (The largest circulated Bengali daily published from Kolkata, New Delhi and Mumbai by ABP Group of publications) and *Bartaman Patrika* (besides Kolkata it is simultaneously published from four towns of West Bengal, namely—Siliguri, Burdwan, Malda and Midnapore). Random sampling technique was followed to record choice of 600 each of bride and bridegroom during the period of January to December 2015.

After tabulation of data bibliometric techniques were used "to analyse quantitatively the properties and behaviour of recorded knowledge."[31] In this study statistical bibliometric technique is followed as it helps to "shed light on the process of written communication and of the nature and course of development of discipline by means of counting and analysing the various facets of written communication."[32] Bradford's law of scattering states "if scientific journals are arranged in order of decreasing productivity of articles on a given subject, they may be divided into a nucleus of periodicals more particularly devoted to the subject and several groups or zones containing the same number of articles as the nucleus, when the number of periodicals in the nucleus and succeeding zones will be as $1{:}n{:}n^2$."[33] The law is used to identify core journals in a single subject field by dividing the articles into three zones each containing the same numbers of articles. The same relationship has been applied here in case of social choice. This study is limited to Bengali matrimonial and within the time frame of January to December 2015.

Analysis

The advertisement published in matrimony of newspaper facilitates the process of arranged marriage. Individual and family attributes of prospective bride and bridegroom are disclosed to marriage market as a means of information sharing and communication process. Data so derived about the choice of bride are tabulated in Tables 4.1–4.3.

Table 4.1: Top choices of bride

Rank	Requirements	Choice (in nos.)	Percentage
1.	Beauty	487	81.17
2.	Education	393	65.50
3.	Age	320	53.33
4.	Fair complexion	206	34.33
5.	Family background	159	26.50
6.	Caste specification	155	25.83
7.	Employment	148	24.67
8.	Height	125	20.83
9.	Residence	104	17.33
10.	No caste bar	82	13.67
11.	No demand	78	13.00
12.	Slim	77	12.83
13.	*Manglik* (Scripturally auspicious)	76	12.67
14.	Photo	75	12.50
15.	Mention of profession	73	12.17
16.	Homely	71	11.83
17.	Cultured	69	11.50
18.	Horoscope	69	11.50
19.	Not employed	64	10.67
20.	Migrated from East Bengal	61	10.17
21.	Efficient in work	57	9.50
22.	Family member	51	8.50
23.	Blood group	43	7.17
24.	Vegetarian	37	6.17
25.	Divorced	33	5.50
26.	Ownership of property	31	5.17
27.	Long hair	28	4.67
28.	Music	23	3.83
29.	Other choices	326	54.33

Source: Anandabazar and Bartaman Patrika.

Beauty is a predominant choice in the case of bride. It is related with fair complex, shape, height etc. The concept of beauty varies depending upon cultural perceptions and aesthetic ideas of the concerned social group. Educational choices of bride have been analysed separately for educational attainment of a bride. It is significant that 77.60 percent choices are graduate (*see* Table 4.2).

Out of employment requirement of bride a significant per cent (n=45) of bridegroom wish for a bride engaged in teaching profession observed during the study. The height varies in the range of 5′2″ to 5′6″ for bride and age requirement in the range of 22-36 years.

Total choices can be categorized into three zones.

Table 4.2: Educational qualification requirements of Bride

Rank	*Qualification*	*Number*	*Percentage*
1	Graduate	305	77.60
2	Postgraduate	68	17.30
3	Bachelor of Technology	8	2.04
4	Doctor	4	1.02
5	Higher Secondary	4	1.02
6	Secondary	4	1.02
	Total	**393**	**100.00**

Source: Anandabazar and Bartaman Patrika.

Table 4.3: Distribution of zones according to socio-economic choices of bride

Zone	*Choice (in no.)*	*No. of requirements*
First	1200	3
Second	1134	9
Third	1187	72

As per Bradford law each zone comprises more or less equal number of choices, i.e. one third of the total number of choices. Sixteen choices in the third zone mentioned, remaining choices (n = 56) included in other choices as these choices are in single digit. In case of choice the number of individual remains more or less same and number of requirements strictly follow Bradford law in first and second zones but in third zone it is 72 instead of 91. The deviation is not great.

Choices of bridegroom have been recorded in Tables 4.4–4.6.

Secured income in the form of government job is a major choice of bridegroom. Well-established means good private job. Residence of bride is also a major choice in the case of employed bridegroom who wishes their partner to work is closed proximity of their working place so that they can lead a conjugal life residing in a common place.

Mention of academic attainment by bridegroom is much less (n = 111) than brides (n = 391). But post-graduation occupies a significant percentage (64%). Here post-graduate includes Master of Business Administration (n = 13) and Master of Technology (n = 11). Age range for bridegroom varies in the range of 26–44 years. Height requirement varies from 5′6″ to 6′01″.

These choices can be segmented into following three zones as shown in Table 4.6.

Table 4.4: Top choices of bridegroom

Rank	*Requirements*	*Choice (in no.)*	*Percentage*
1	Employment (Government)	310	51.67
2	Age	227	37.83
3	Residence	203	33.83
4	Well-established	199	33.17
5	Education	111	18.50
6	Caste specification	87	14.50
7	Business/private job	71	11.83
8	Height	58	9.67
9	Beauty	41	6.83
10	Family background	37	6.17
11	No demand	35	5.83
12	No caste bar	33	5.50
13	Business	32	5.33
14	Good character	31	5.17
15	Good earning	31	5.17
16	Divorced	30	5.00
17	No drug addiction	29	4.83
18	Good health	27	4.50
19	Fair complex	26	4.33
20	Blood group	24	4.00
21	Cultured	23	3.83
22	Doctor	23	3.83
23	Engineer	21	3.50
24	Horoscope	21	3.50
25	Ownership of property	19	3.17
26	Vegetarian	17	2.83
27	Photo	14	2.33
28	*Mangalik* (Scripturally auspicious)	11	1.83
29	Other choices	330	55.00

Source: Anandabazar and Bartaman Patrika.

Table 4.5: Educational qualification requirements of bridegroom

Rank	*Qualification*	*Number*	*Percentage*
1.	Graduate	15	13.51
2.	Postgraduate	71	63.96
3.	Bachelor of Technology	17	15.32
4.	Doctor	5	4.51
5.	Advocate	3	2.70
	Total	**111**	**100.00**

Here again choice of bridegroom follows Bradford law. Sixteen choices in the third zone mentioned, remaining choices (n = 57) included in other choices. The core choice (zone 1) of bride and bridegroom varies for brides—it is beauty—education and age;

Table 4.6: Distribution of zones according to socio-economic choice of bridegroom

Zone	Choice (in no.)	No. of requirements
First	740	3
Second	672	9
Third	709	73

for bridegroom—it is employment, age and residence. Here also number of requirements in zones 1 and 2 strictly follows Bradford law, and marginally varies in zone 3.

As a means of communication out of total 1200 samples 717 (i.e. 59.75%) mentioned phone no. 458 (i.e. 38.17%) used e-mail address as well as phone number; only mail (n = 16) and only postal address (n = 9). It signifies that postal communication has lost its credential as a means of communication. Telecommunication and information communication technology take a lead role in communication.

Discussion

From this study one can identify ranks of social choices relating to bride and bridegroom. If it is compared with the sociological surveys of Indian women like *She who rides a peacock* (1960)[34]; *Towards equality* (1974)[35] or more recent study on *Debating patriarchy* (2012)[36] the substantial changes in social choice can be noticed such as education in India has gone through a sea change. In pre-British period the large numbers of indigenous schools were religious in character and regarded knowledge as a means of spiritual growth. British introduced a new system of education "... to form a class who may be interpreters between us [British] and the millions whom we [British] govern, a class of persons Indian in blood and colour, but English in tastes, opinions, morals and intellect."[37] But now it can safely be stated that anywhere in India the need of education of girls as much as boys is recognized as a cardinal need of progress—*A sine qua non* of national progress. Now, it is believed that girls will be able to get better husband and can earn money to secure their life and support family members.

Due to moving of the society from agricultural to industrial plus urbanization, the former tightly structured caste system is gradually breaking down. Prestigious hierarchy in the social system based on caste is changing to job-oriented status. The age of marriage of both men and women in India has varied from time to time and region to region as well as with religion, caste and language differences. The old practice of child marriage has been abolished with the enactment of Child Marriage Restraint Act, 1929. Now, the age of marriage has gone up. This is mainly due to "the difficulty of securing jobs by persons of low educational qualifications has driven more and more persons to seek higher education and higher education has invariably meant comparatively late marriage."[38] So, girls may marry now as late as twenty-five years of age without too much criticism from family and friends. The ages of brides and bridegrooms increases due to getting a job at late age and ultimate settling down through trial and error methods.

Personal appearance of brides matters as men wanted beautiful wives. Beauty has been described as 'moderately' beautiful to 'real beauty', 'fair' etc. Fair-skinned brides have been considered of great importance in India through the ages. Women's relative lack of interest in the appearance of their future husbands fits with the relative unimportance of men's looks in India. The caste system in India was never a static one; it has undergone change with new castes and sub-castes and in the prestige ranking in caste hierarchy. Its tagging with caste occupation has changed with the shifting of society for agrarian to urban. As a result men are now more inclined to lenient attitude to inter-caste and inter-racial marriage. Social prestige now largely depends upon educational attainment, employment and earning capacity.

Conclusion

It is clear from the study that socio-economic choice in matrimonial strictly follows Bradford law in zones 1 and 2, but varies slightly in zone 3. Maybe, it is due to lack of scope of expression of choice in mass media. So, there is possibility that the law is found to be fitting in many other social science phenomena as well. Comparative study on matrimonial choice in different decades and application of Bradford law can focus more light not only to identify core social choices in different zones, but also shifting of choice with changes of society through the ages. Thus, it can pave a new way of social research. Matrimonial advertisements in the media can reveal the changing notions of feminity and its negotiations with economic realities and practical value system.

References

1. MacIver, R.M. and Page, Charles H., (2006), *Society an Introductory Analysis*. Delhi: MacMillan India, p. 5.
2. Arnold, W., Green (1952), *An Analysis of Life in Modern Society*. New York: McGraw-Hill, p. 370.
3. Karve, I., (1953), *Kingship Organisation in India*. Poona: Deccan College, p. 10.
4. Coontz, S., (2005), *Marriage: A History*. New York: Vikings.
5. Karve, I., (1953), *Kingship Organisation in India*. Poona: Deccan College, p. 7.
6. Bradford, S.C. (1934) Sources of Information on Specific Subjects. *Engineering*. 137(3550): 85-86.
7. Brookes, B.C. (1977) Theory of Bradford's law. *Journal of Documentation*. 33(3): 180-209.
8. Qui, L. (1990) An empirical examination of the existing model for Bradford's law. *Information Processing and Management*. 26(5): 655-672.
9. Egghe, L. (1986) The dual of Bradford's law. *Journal of American Society of Information Science*. 37: 173-189.
10. Leimkuhler, Ferdinand F. (1967) The Bradford distribution. *Journal of Documentation*. 23(3): 197-207.
11. Chen, Y.S.; Chong, P.P. and Tong, M.Y. (1995) Dynamic behaviour of Bradford's law. *Journal of the American Society for Information Science*. 46(5): 370-383.
12. Rao, I.K.R. (1998) An analysis of Bradford multipliers and a model to explain law of scattering. *Scientometrics*. 41(1-2): 93-100.
13. Nicolasian, J. and Hjorland, B. (2007) Practical potentials of Bradford's law: a critical examination of the received view. *Journal of Documentation*. 63(3): 359-377.
14. Rao, I.K.R., 1972, Dispersion of documents on survey analysis, Bradford and Pareto distribution. *Library Science with a Slant to Documentation*. 9(3): 396-403.
15. Lawani, S.M. (1973) Bradford's Law and the Literature of Agriculture. *International Library Review*. 5(3): 341-50.
16. Drott, M.C. and Griffith, B.C. (1978) An empirical examination of Bradford's law and the scattering of scientific literature. *Journal of American Society of Information Science*. 29(5): 238-46.
17. Heine, M.H. (1998) Bradford ranking conventions and their application to a growing literature. *Journal of Documentation*. 54(3): 303-331.
18. Ram, S. and Paliwal, N. (2014) Assessment of Bradford law of scattering to Psoriasis literature through bibliometric snapshot. *DESIDOC Journal of Library & Information Technology*. 34(1): 46-56.
19. Egghe, L. (1990) Application of the theory of Bradford's law to the

calculation of Leimkuhler's law and the completion of bibliographies. *Journal of American Society for Information Science.* 41(3): 204-09.

20. Lal, A. and Panda, K.C. (1999) Bradford's law and its application to bibliography of plant pathology dissertation: an analytical approach. *Library Science with a Slant to Documentation and Information Studies.* 36(3): 193-206.
21. Velmurugan, C. and Radhakrishnan, N. (2005), Application of Bradford's law of scattering to the scientific publications of energy and environment research. *Engineering International.* 3(2): 75-86.
22. Garudadwajan, B. and Murthy, H. S. S. (1969) Bradford distribution-an application to the study of core collection of periodical in aeronautics and related subjects. *Library Science with a Slant to Documentation.* 20(3): 159-90.
23. Goffman, W. and Morris, T.G. (1970), Bradford's law and library acquisitions. *Nature.* (226) (5249): 922-923.
24. Drott, M.C.; Mancall, J.C. and Griffith, B.C. (1979) Bradford's law and libraries: present applications—potential promise. *Aslib Proceedings. 31*(6): 296-304.
25. Tyagi, A.K. (1986) Bradford's Law and its application to study citation frequency of bibliographical data of *Indian Journal of Physics. ILA Bulletin.* 21(3-4): 90-95.
26. Gupta, D.K. (1991) Application of Bradford's law to citation data of *Ethiopian Medical Journal. Annals of Library Science and Documentation.* 38(3): 85-98.
27. Singh, K.P., and Bebi, (2014) Application of Bradford's law on journal citation: a study of Ph.D. theses in Social Sciences of University of Delhi. *Annals of Library and Information Studies.* 61 (2): 112-120.
28. Sen, B.K. (2015) Ranked list and zonal distribution of periodicals in Bradford law. *Annals of Library and Information Studies.* 62(1): 48-50.
29. Bandyopadhyay, A. (1999) Bradford's law in different disciplines. *Annals of Library Science and Documentation.* 46(4): 133-138.
30. Ray, P. P. and Sen, B.K. (2012) Letter correspondence of Rabindranath Tagore: a study. *Annals of Library and Information Studies.* 59(2): 122-127.
31. Pritchard, A. (1969) Statistical bibliography or bibliometrics. *Journal of Documentation.* 24(4): 348.
32. Hulme, E.W. (1923), *Statistical Bibliography in Relation to Growth of Modern Civilization.* London: Grafton, p. 44.
33. Bradford, S.C., (1953), *Documentation.*London: Crossby Lockwood, p. 154.
34. Cormack, M., (1961), *She who Rides a Peacock.*London: Social Change.
35. India, (1974) *Towards Equality: Report of the Status of Women in India.* New Delhi: Ministry of Education and Social Welfare.

36. Sinha, C., (2012), *Debating Patriarchy: The Hindu Code Bill Controversy in India (1941-1956)*. New Delhi: Oxford University Press, p. 230.
37. Mukherji, D.P., (1948), *Modern Indian Culture: A Sociological Study*, 2nd edn. Bombay: Hind Kitabs, p. 78.
38. Census of India, 1950, vol. XIV, Part 1. Bangalore: Director of Printing, Stationery and Publications, 1954, pp. 107-108.

5
Creativity of Satyajit Ray
A Bibliometric Study

Introduction

Satyajit Ray (1921-1992) son of Sukumar Ray and Suprova Devi was born on 2nd May, 1921 in Calcutta (now Kolkata). The family was *"... a distinguished family of artists and intellectuals whose prominence in Indian art and literature could be traced back to fifteen generations."*[1] After completing honours degree in Economics from Presidency College, Calcutta, he was sent to Santiniketan, a school founded by Rabindranath Tagore for all-round education. The education values of learning from nature and craft based education helped to build an 'ambivalent' relationship with Santiniketan. The place opened windows for him and make him aware about Indian tradition, values and ethos which lays the foundation of creation of art and culture.

Satyajit Ray popularly known as film director started his career as a junior visualiser. Ray met French film director Jean Renoir in 1949 who visited Calcutta to shoot his film *'The River'* (1951) and his visit to England in 1950 had a great influence on his film career. Ray saw Vittorio de Sica's *'Ladri di biciclette'* (Bicycle Thief) at his arrival in England and his contact with Lindsay Anderson and Gavin Lambert inspired Ray to become a film maker.[2] Ray made his directorial debut in 1955 with *Pather Panchali* from the novel of Bibhutibhusan Banerjee, a well known literary personality in Bengal. Besides film direction Ray composed music, wrote screenplays, illustrator, calligrapher. He also authored several short stories and novels in Bengali mainly for children and adolescents.

Satyajit Ray received numerous awards in recognisation of his creation. It includes National and International Film Awards and honorary Academy Awards. Ray was awarded with India's highest honour in cinema the *Dadasaheb Phalke* Award in 1984 and highest civilian award *Bharat Ratna* in 1992. He is the recipient of Doctor of letters from as many as seven Indian Universities and also from University of Oxford; Royal College of Art, London; Academy of Motion Picture, Arts and Sciences, USA (awarded honorary Oscar in 1992 for lifetime achievement). He was awarded from International Film Festivals of Chicago (1973), Berlin (1978), Moscow (1979), Canner (1981), Tokyo (1991) and San Francisco (1992).[3]

Bibliography on different aspects of Satyajit Ray, such as publication, filmography etc. has been compiled. But no efforts has yet been made for a comprehensive study considering his total intellectual output from the point of view of information science. But quantitative and qualitative studies of productivity of a creator with proper graphical representation help to analyse and understand his/her contribution in proper perspective.[4-6] For measuring productivity output, channel of communication of scientists scientometric studies have been carried out on the works of Nobel Laureate[7-15] scientists as well as eminent scientists.[16-22] But for quantitative analysis of publication profile of social scientists, bibliometric techniques[23-25] had been applied. Here this technique has been followed to measure production output of versatile genius Satyajit Ray.

Objectives

- To measure quantitatively Satyajit Ray's contribution to literature and filmography;
- To find out year-wise growth of publication and filmography;
- To identify core communication channels for publication of articles; and
- To find out collaborator and their association with Ray's filmography.

Methodology of the Study

Bibliometric study on individual scholars to find out productivity coefficient, publication density, publication concentration requires compilation of bibliography for quantitative and qualitative documentation of an individual scholar. A comprehensive bibliography consisting of books, articles (both in Bengali and English language) and films produced by Ray's were compiled in chronological order from different sources.[26-29] The bibliography includes all publications during his lifetime and posthumous publications in one chronological sequence as well as films and screenplays. The year of publication or production (in case of films) has been considered as contribution in a particular year. Present study is limited to books, articles, films produced by Ray.

Results

Satyajit Ray authored sixty one (n = 61) books including fifteen (n = 15) posthumous publications. Ray's most novels and stories first published in Bengali notable periodicals *Sandesh, Desh* or *Anandamela*. Then they were published in book form mostly by Ananda Publisher, Kolkata. His first book published in 1967 is a book on science fantasies *Professor Shonku*. Second book a detective one *Badsahi Angti* published in 1969 by Ananda Publisher which has been reprinted more than 50 times. Posthumous publications are mostly collection of detective stories character *'Feluda'* or science fantasies character *'Professor Shonku'*. His stories are unpretentious and entertaining. The subjects included: adventure, detective stories, fantasy, science fiction and even horror (*see* Table 5.1).

The productivity coefficient could be obtained by the simple formula of 50 percentile age per total productivity age. Fifty percentile age is the number of years during which 50 per cent of the papers (books in this study) were published starting from the year of publication of the first paper. Productivity age on the other hand is the count from the year in which first paper by an author was published till the last year of publication.[30] Ray's productivity coefficient for books is 2.21 (where 50 percentile age is 64 and publishing age is 29 including posthumous publications).

Published screenplays of Satyajit Ray stands to thirty nine (n = 39) comprising both Bengali (n = 29) and English (n = 10) plays. The published screenplays often differ significantly from the screenplays of the films. First screenplay in Bengali was *Postmaster*[31] published in 1961. In the same year first English screenplay also published was Rabindranath Tagore.[32] The last publication is a posthumous one *The stranger* (*see* Fig. 5.1).[33]

Table 5.1: Chronological distribution of books

Author's age	*Year*	*No. of Publications*	*Cumulative total*	*Publishing ag(*
46	1967	1	1	1
48	1969	1	2	2
49	1970	3	5	3
50	1971	2	7	4
52	1973	1	8	5
53	1974	2	10	6
54	1975	1	11	7
55	1976	5	16	8
56	1977	1	17	9
58	1979	3	20	10
59	1980	2	22	11
60	1981	3	25	12
61	1982	2	27	13
62	1983	2	29	14
63	1984	1	30	15
64	1985	3	33	16
65	1986	2	35	17
66	1987	6	41	18
67	1988	1	42	19
68	1989	1	43	20
70	1991	1	44	21
71	1992	2	46	22
72	1993	1	47	23
73	1994	4	51	24
74	1995	2	53	25
75	1996	3	56	26
77	1998	2	58	27
79	2000	2	60	28
81	2002	1	61	29

Source: Author.

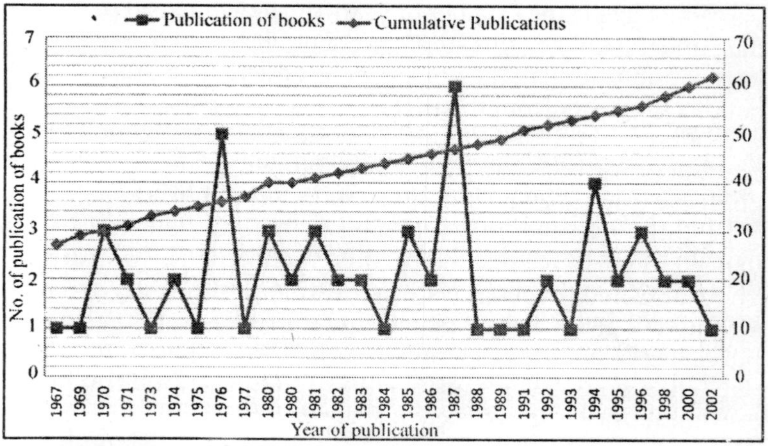

Fig. 5.1: Publication produc' ity of books

Table 5.2: Chronological distribution of screenplays

Author's age	*Year*	*No. of publications*	*Cumulative total*	*Publishing age*
40	1961	2	2	1
43	1964	1	3	2
44	1965	1	4	3
45	1966	2	6	4
48	1969	1	7	5
51	1972	2	9	6
52	1973	2	11	7
55	1976	1	12	8
57	1978	1	13	9
59	1980	1	14	10
60	1981	3	17	11
61	1982	3	20	12
62	1983	2	22	13
63	1984	2	24	14
64	1985	2	26	15
65	1986	1	27	16
66	1987	2	29	17
67	1988	1	30	18
68	1989	2	32	19
69	1990	1	33	20
70	1991	1	34	21
71	1992	1	35	22
72	1993	1	36	23
73	1994	1	37	24
77	1998	1	38	25
82	2003	1	39	26

Ray's productivity coefficient for screenplays stands to 2.35 (where 50 percentile age is 61 and publishing age is 26 including posthumous publications)(*see* Fig. 5.2).

Satyajit Ray wrote articles both in English (n = 69) and Bengali (n = 53) language. The articles deal with different aspects of films as well as social, cultural aspects. Out of 69 articles in English language 25 deal with different aspects of films. First two articles in English published in *Statesman* in August 1948 were *"What is wrong in Indian films"* and *"National styles in the cinema."* The last one was on Rabindranath Tagore entitled *"The home and the world"* published in *Guardian*, 1 August, 1991 (*see* Table 5.3).

Productivity coefficient for English articles of Satyajit is 48/34, i.e., 1.41 (where 48 is 50 percentile age and 34 is total productivity age).

Ray chose 30 communication channels to communicate his 69 articles during the period 1948-1991. *Statesman* is the most frequently (n = 11) used channel of communication which covers

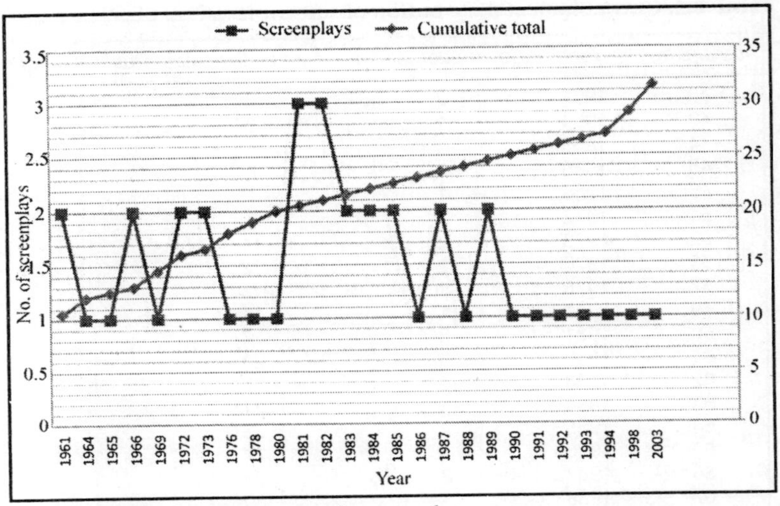

Fig. 5.2: Productivity output of screenplays

15.94 per cent of his articles. Thus, Ray considers popular mass communication channel to communicate his ideas. Remaining are mostly journals devoted to films (*see* Table 5.4).

Publication density[34] is defined as the ratio of total number of papers published to the total number of journals in which papers were published. Publication density of Ray's articles is found to be 69/30, i.e. 2.30. Publication concentration on the other hand is the ratio in percentage of the channels having half of the papers published to the total number of journals in which those papers were published. Ray published his papers in English in 30 channels among which seven channels, namely Statesman (n = 11); *New York Times* and *Indian Film Culture* (n = 5 each); *Film World and Souvenir* (n = 4 each); *Sight and Sound* and *Montage* (n = 3 each) covers more than half of the articles. Hence, publication concentration of short stories would be: 7/30 × 100 = 23.33.

Ray's articles written in Bengali language also deals with *Chalachchitra* (film) as well as other areas. Out of 53 articles in Bengali 18 in the period of 1955-1980 devoted to films. First two articles of 1955 were on films, namely: *Oraphe Indir Thakrun* (*Alias* Indir Thakrun) published in *Madhyabitta* and *Pather Panchali prasange* (On Pather Panchali) published in *Sanko*. The last two articles were posthumous publication. One is his speech at a

Table 5.3: Chronological distribution of articles (English)

Author's age	*Year*	*No. of publications*	*Cumulative total*	*Publishing age*
27	1948	1	1	1
28	1949	1	2	2
29	195	1	3	3
3	1951	1	4	4
35	1956	1	5	5
36	1957	3	8	6
37	1958	2	1	7
39	196	1	11	8
41	1962	2	13	9
42	1963	3	16	1
43	1964	5	21	11
44	1965	2	23	12
45	1966	7	3	13
46	1967	3	33	14
47	1968	1	34	15
48	1969	3	37	16
49	197	4	41	17
5	1971	1	42	18
51	1972	2	44	19
52	1973	1	45	2
53	1974	4	49	21
54	1975	1	5	22
55	1976	3	53	23
57	1978	1	54	24
59	198	3	57	25
61	1982	3	6	26
62	1983	1	61	27
63	1984	1	62	28
64	1985	1	63	29
65	1986	1	64	3
66	1987	1	65	31
67	1988	1	66	32
68	1989	1	67	33
7	1991	2	69	34

memorial meeting for Bengali legendry film artist Uttam Kumar in 1980 published in *Chitravash* in 1993 as *Uttam Kumar smarane*. The last one is on another famous film director Ritwik Ghatak entitled *Ritwik maneprane Bengali parichalak* (Ritwik in heart and soul a Bengali director) published in *Bijnapanparba*, 1994 (*see* Table 5.5).

Productivity coefficient for Bengali articles of Satyajit is 48/28, i.e. 1.71 (where 48 is 50 percentile age and 28 is total productivity age.

Table 5.4: Channel-wise scattering of articles (English)

Sl.No.	*Channel*	*No. of publications*	*FPY*	*LPY*	*%*
1.	Statesman	11	1948	1982	15.94
2.	Sequence	2	1950	1970	2.90
3.	Calcutta Film Soc. Bul.	2	1951	1964	2.90
4.	Indian Film Quarterly	1	1957	1957	1.45
5.	Sight and Sound	3	1957	1982	4.35
6.	Amrita Bazar Patrika	1	1957	1957	1.45
7.	Mainstream	2	1962	1963	2.90
8.	New York Times	5	1963	1967	7.25
9.	Indian Film Culture	5	1963	1974	7.25
10	Kino	1	1964	1964	1.45
11.	Now	3	1964	1969	4.35
12.	Link	1	1966	1966	1.45
13.	Montage	3	1966	1967	4.35
14.	Film World	4	1968	1970	5.80
15.	Souvenir	4	1969	1976	5.80
16.	Magazine (St. Xavier's College)	1	1970	1970	1.45
17.	Span	1	1970	1970	1.45
18.	Film fare	3	1971	1972	4.35
19.	Communicator: Jls. of Indian Instt. of Mass Communication	1	1974	1974	1.45
20.	Jls. of the National Institute of (Film Bul. of Chalachchitram)	1	1976	1976	1.45
21.	Tenth Muse Performing Art	1	1976	1976	1.45
22.	Illustrated Weekly of India	1	1978	1978	1.45
23.	Cinema Vision India	2	1980	1980	2.90
24.	Sunday	1	1980	1980	1.45
25.	Telegraph	2	1982	1991	2.90
26.	Brochure	3	1983	1989	4.35
27.	Sunday Observer	1	1985	1985	1.45
28.	Cinema in India	1	1987	1987	1.45
29.	Chaplin (Stockholm)	1	1988	1988	1.45
30.	Guardian	1	1991	1991	1.45
	Total	**69**	**1948**	**1991**	**100.00**

Source: Author.

For communicating Bengali articles Satyajit used 24 channels. Most frequently used channel of communication is *Eksan* and *Sandesh* (n = 6 each). Ray himself was editor of *Sandesh* for eight years (1915-1923). Ray also designed cover page of many issues of both the journals (*see* Table 5.6).

Publication density for papers written in Bengali is 53/24, i.e. 2.21. Publication concentration would be: 4/24 × 100 = 16.67 (out of 24 channels 4 channels namely Desh (n = 14), *Eksan* (n = 6), *Sandesh* (n = 6) and *Anandabazar Patrika* (n = 3) covers half of the papers published).

Table 5.5: Chronological distribution of articles (Bengali)

Author's age	*Year*	*No. of publications*	*Cumulative total*	*Publishing age*
34	1955	2	2	1
38	1959	2	4	2
39	1960	1	5	3
41	1962	2	7	4
42	1963	2	9	5
43	1964	3	12	6
44	1965	1	13	7
45	1966	2	15	8
46	1967	6	21	9
47	1968	4	25	10
48	1969	2	27	11
49	1970	1	28	12
50	1971	1	29	13
51	1972	2	31	14
52	1973	1	32	15
53	1974	2	34	16
54	1975	1	35	17
55	1976	2	37	18
57	1978	2	39	19
58	1979	3	42	20
59	1980	1	43	21
60	1981	2	45	22
61	1982	1	46	23
62	1983	1	47	24
66	1987	2	49	25
68	1989	2	51	26
72	1993	1	52	27
73	1994	1	53	28

Source: Author.

Satyajit Ray directed 36 films, including 29 feature films, five documentaries and two short films. Ray also contributed in 19 films directed by others in the period of 1948-1994 either as script writer or music director. The last one produced in 1994 was *Uttoran* (The Broken Journey) produced by his son Sandip Ray. Satyajit wrote the screenplay. Top four producers of his film producing 19 films were: Government of India (n = 6), R.D.B. & Co. (R.D. Bansal) (n = 5), Government of West Bengal and S.R. Production (n = 4 each). On the other hand in photography Soumendu Roy was associated in 21 films (1961-1984) and Subrata Mitra for 10 films (1955-1966). Dulal Dutta edited all the 36 films produced by Satyajit during 1955-1991. As Art Director Bansi Chandragupta contributed most (n = 20) during 1955-1977 and Asok Bose (n = 12) during 1971-1991. Durgadas Mitra alone was associated in 7 films during

Table 5.6: Channel-wise scattering of articles (Bengali)

Sl. No.	Channel	No. of publications	FPY	LPY	%
1.	Sanko	1	1955	1955	1.89
2.	Madhyabitta	1	1955	1955	1.89
3.	Desh	14	1959	1974	26.41
4.	Chalachchitra	1	1959	1959	1.89
5.	Betar Jagat	1	1960	1960	1.89
6.	Booklet (Sadharan Brahmo Samaj)	1	1962	1962	1.89
7.	Prabandha Patrika	1	1963	1963	1.89
8.	Anandabazar Patrika	3	1963	1979	5.66
9.	Parichay	2	1964	1976	3.77
10.	Chitrapat	1	1966	1966	1.89
11.	Cinema Samalochana	1	1966	1966	1.89
12.	Eksan	6	1967	1989	11.32
13.	Sandesh	6	1967	1989	11.32
14.	Bharatkosh	1	1967	1967	1.89
15.	Chitrabiksan	1	1968	1968	1.89
16.	Anvesa	1	1972	1972	1.89
17.	Antarjatik Angik	1	1973	1973	1.89
18.	Mahaagar	1	1974	1974	1.89
19.	Chitravash	3	1976	1993	5.66
20.	Anandolok	2	1978	1980	3.77
21.	Samatat	1	1979	1979	1.89
22.	Bibhab	1	1979	1979	1.89
23.	Kalpaniijhar	1	1981	1981	1.89
24.	Bijnapanparba	1	1994	1994	1.89
	Total	**53**	**1955**	**1994**	**100.00**

Source: Author.

1956-67 and jointly with J.D. Irani in 5 films during 1970-1975 as sound director. Satyajit screen plays include fiction/story of Bengali writers (n = 33) except *Shatranj ke Khilari* (The Chess Players) and *Sadgati* (Deliverance) of Premchand and *Ganasatru* (An Enemy of the People) of Henrik Ibsen produced in 1989. Screen plays from his writings in 14 occasions (*see* Table 5.7).[35]

Productivity coefficient for Filmography is 49/30, i.e. 1.63 (where 49 is 50 percentile age and 30 is total productivity age) which significantly high for producer of his statures.

Conclusion

It is very difficult to justify multifaceted versatility personality in a single study. This is particularly true in the case of a creative artist as well as literary personality like Satyajit Ray. In his creation

Table 5.7: Chronological distribution of Filmography

Author's age	*Year*	*No. of production*	*Cumulative total*	*Publishing age*
34	1955 (Pather Panchali)	1	1	1
35	1956 (Aparajita)	1	2	2
37	1958 (Parash Pathar; Jalsabhar)	2	4	3
38	1959 (Apur Sansar)	1	5	4
39	1960 (Devi)	1	6	5
40	1961 (Tin Kanya: Rabindranath Tagore)	2	8	6
41	1962 (Kanchanjangha: Abhijan)	2	10	7
42	1963 (Mahanagar)	1	11	8
43	1964 (Charulata:Two)	2	13	9
44	1965 (Kapurush-O-Mahapurush)	1	14	10
45	1966 (Nayak)	1	15	11
46	1967 (Chiriakhana)	1	16	12
47	1968 (Goopy Gyne Bagha Byne)	1	17	13
48	1969 (Aranyer Din Ratri)	1	18	14
49	1970 (Pratidwandi)	1	19	15
50	1971 (Seemabaddha: Sikkim)	2	21	16
51	1972 (The Inner Eye)	1	22	17
52	1973 (Asani Sanket)	1	23	18
53	1974 (Sonar Kella)	1	24	19
54	1975 (Jana Aranya)	1	25	20
55	1976 (Bala)	1	26	21
56	1977 (Shatranj Ke Khilari)	1	27	22
57	1978 (Joi Baba Felunath)	1	28	23
59	1980 (Hirak Rajar Deshe: Pikoo)	2	30	24
60	1981 (Sadgati)	1	31	25
63	1984 (Ghare Baire)	1	32	26
66	1987 (Sukumar Ray)	1	33	27
68	1989 (Ganasatru)	1	34	28
69	1990 (Sakha Prasakha)	1	35	29
70	1991 (Agantuk)	1	36	30

large truth has been expressed in small details. Actually the whole business of creation, of the ideas that come in a flash, cannot be explained by science. It cannot. The best ideas come at moments when one is not even thinking of it. Ray's film covers all sections of society and works of life. But Ray observes "The most distinctive feature of my films is that they are deeply rooted in Bengal, in Bengali culture, mannerisms and mores. What makes them universal in appeal is that they are about human beings."[36]

Short stories and novels authored by Ray are mainly meant for children and adolescents. Characters created by him like *Feluda* and *Professor Shonku* has a great impact on the mind of youth and adolescent even today as detective story and science fantasies. Most of the books authored by him had been reprinted quite several times[37] indicate the popularity of his books. The secret is exposed by him "When I write my own story, I use characters and milieus I am familiar with."[38] "His work has a tempo and rhythm which are most effective in expressing themselves. They are not "slow" at all. It can be described as flowering composedly, like a big river."[39]

In his direction, writing, sketch, composition of music (Ray composed music for all the films produced by him except first six) in a word his creative mind was greatly influenced by Santiniketan education. Universal humanitarian appeal of his movies influenced people throughout the world. He himself observed "Shantiniketan made me the combined product of East and West that I am. As a film-maker I owe as much to Shantiniketan as I do to American and European cinema."[40] Oscar citation rightly mentioned Ray as "rare mastery of the art of motion pictures", "profound humanitarian outlook" and "indelible influence on film-makers and audiences throughout the world."[41]

References

1. Banerjee, S., (1996), *Satyajit Ray beyond the Frame*. New Delhi: Allied Publishers, p. 6.
2. Robinson, A., (1989), *Satyajit Ray: The Inner Eye*. London: I.B. Tauris, pp. 56-58.
3. https://en.wikipedia.org/wiki/List_of_awards_and_nominations_received_by_Satyajit_Ray (Visited on 23 Febuary, 2016).
4. Kalyane, V. L. and Vidyasagar Rao, K. (1995) Quantification of credits for authorship. *ILA Bulletin*. 30(3-4): 94-96.
5. Sen, S.K. and Gan, S.K. (1990) Biobibliometrics: Concept and application in the study of productivity of scientists. *International Forum on Information and Documentation*. 15(3): 13-21.
6. Durieux, Van and G.P.A. (2010) Bibliometric Indicators, Quality Measurements of Scientific Publication. *Radiology*. 25(5): 342-351.
7. Gupta, D.K. (1999) Chandrasekhar: winner of the Nobel Prize for physics: a citation analysis of his work. *Annals of Library and Information Studies*. 30(14): 177-184.
8. Kademani, B.S.; Kalyane, V.L. and Jange, S. (1999) Scientometric portrait of Nobel Laureate Dorothy Crowfoot Hodgkin. *Scientometrics*. 45 (2): 233-250.

9. Kademani, B.S.; Kalyane, V.L. and Kademani, A.B. (1994) Scientometric portrait of Nobel Laureate Dr. C.V. Raman. *Indian Journal of Information, Library and Society*. 7 (3-4): 215-249.
10. Kademani, B.S.; Kalyane, V.L. (1996) and Kademani, A.B. Scientometric portrait of Nobel Laureate S. Chandrasekhar. *JISSI: The International Journal of Scientometrics and Informetrics*. 2 (2-3): 119-135.
11. Kademani, B.S.; Kalyane, V.L. and Kumar, V. (2002) Scientometric portrait of Nobel Laureate Harold W. Kroto. *SRELS Journal of Information Management*. 39 (4): 409-434.
12. Kademani, B.S.; Kalyane, V.L. and Kumar, V. (2002) Scientometric portrait of Nobel Laureate Ahmed Hassan Zewail. *Malaysian Journal of Library and Information Science*. 6 (2): 53-70.
13. Kalyane, V.L. and Kademani, B.S. (1997) Scientometric portrait of Barbara McClintock: the Nobel Laureate in Physiology. *Kelpro Bulletin*. 1 (1). 3-14.
14. Kalyane, V.L. and Sen, B.K. (1996) Scientometric portrait of Nobel Laureate Pierre-Gilles de Gennes. *Malaysian Journal of Library and Information Science*. 1 (2): 13-26.
15. Koganuramath, M.M., *et al.*, (2004): Nobel Laureate Wolfgang Ketterle: a scientometric portrait. *Malaysian Journal of Library and Information Science*. 9 (2): 35-61.
16. Hazarika, T. S.; Sarma, D. and Sen, B.K. (2010) Scientometric portrait of Nayana Nanda Borthakur: a biometeorologist. *Annals of Library and Information Studies*. 57 (1): 21-32.
17. Kademani, B.S.; Kalyane, V.L. (1996) Bibliometric indicators of publication productivity analysis of an individual scientist. *JISSI: The International Journal of Scientometrics and Informetrics*. 2(4): 49-58.
18. Kademani, B.S.; Kalyane, V.L. and Balakrishnan, M.R. (1994) Scientometric portrait of P.K. Iyengar. *Library Science*. 31(4): 155-176.
19. Kademani, B.S.; Kalyane, V.L. and Kademani, A.B. (1996) Scientometric portrait of Sir K.S. Krishnan. *Indian Journal of Information Library and Society*. 9 (1-2): 125-150.
20. Kademani, B.S.; Kalyane, V.S. and Kumar, V. (2000) Scientometric portrait of Vikram Ambalal Sarabhai: a citation analysis. *SRELS Journal of Information Management*. 37(2): 107-132.
21. Kademani, B.S. Surwase, G. and Kumar, V. (2009) Bhabha Scattering: a scientometric view. *DESIDOC Journal of Library & Information Technology*. 29(4): 3-11.
22. Kalyane, V.L. and Kademani, B.S. (1995) Scientometric portrait of R. Chidambaram: a publication productivity analysis. *Journal of Information Sciences*. 5(3): 101-140.
23. Sinha, S.C. and Ullah, M.F. (1994) Information profile of an Indian bibliometrician: Bibliometric study of Dr. I.N. Sengupta's publications. *Indian Journal of Information, Library and Society*. 7 (3-4): 250-261.

24. Tiew, W.S. and Khoo, Kay Kim (1999) Professor of Malaysian history: a bibliometric study. *Malaysian Journal of Library and Information Science*. 4 (2): 47-57.
25. Ray, P.P. and Sen, B.K. (2015) Publication of Rabindranath Tagore: a bibliometric study. *Annals of Library and Information Studies*. 62 (3): 177-186.
26. Banerjee, S., (1996), *Satyajit Ray beyond the Frame*. Calcutta: Allied Publishers, pp. 215-222.
27. Robinson, A., (2005), *Satyajit Ray: A Vision of Cinema*. London: I.B. Tauris, pp. 327-352.
28. Das, S., (1998), *Satyajit Ray: An Intimate Master*. Calcutta: Allied Publishers.
29. https://en.wikipedia.org/wiki/Satyajit_Ray_filmography (Visited on 23 Febuary, 2016).
30. Sen, S.K. and Gan, S.K. (1990), Bibliometrics: concept and application in the study of productivity of scientists. *International Forum on Information and Documentation*. 15 (3): 13-21.
31. Ray, S. (1961), The Postmaster. *Chalachchitra*, 1(3).
32. Ray, S., (1961), Portrait of a man. *UNESCO Courier*, Paris, December.
33. Ray, S., (2003), *The Stranger*. New Delhi: TLM Books.
34. Vinkler, P., (1990), *Bibliometric Analysis of Publication Activity of a Scientific Research Institute*. Amsterdam: Elsevier, pp. 309-334.
35. Robinson, A., (1989), *Satyajit Ray: The Inner Eye*. London: I.B. Tauris, pp. 327-351.
36. Ray, S., Interview, *Time*, 6 January, 1992.
37. www.parabaas.com/satyajit/articles/bibliography.html (visited on 23 Febuary, 2016)
38. Ray, S., (1976), *Our Films Their Films*. Delhi: Orient Longman, p. 64.
39. Robinson, A., (1989), *Satyajit Ray: The Inner Eye*. London: I.B. Tauris, p. 282.
40. Ray, S., (1 August, 1991), The Home and the World, *Guardian*.
41. Banerjee, S., (1996), *Satyajit Ray beyond the Frame*. New Delhi: Allied Publishers, p. 21.

SECTION II

Tagoreana

6

Publications of Tagoreana Before and After Expiry of Copyright

A Study

Introduction

Rabindranath is known to the world for his extraordinary quality and versatility as a poet. But, he also left his undeniable mark moved on other areas as a playwright, novelist, philosopher, composer and singer, innovator in education and rural development, actor, director and painter, cultural ambassador and what not. Rabindranath, more than any other person in history, illustrated what in the Italian renaissance was called the archetype of *l'uomo universale* (the universal man). His inheritance belongs to mankind, but the presence of his many splendoured geniuses is ubiquitously felt at his experimental school at *Santiniketan* (Abode of Peace) and rural reconstruction programme at *Sriniketan* (Abode of Sri Lakshmi). As recognition for his contribution to literature Rabindranath was awarded with the Nobel Prize in the year 1913.

Rabindranath gave copyright of all his works to Visva-Bharati. The first volume of *Vichitra Prabanda* (Miscellaneous Essays), published in 1907 with the declaration "the copyright of these works rest with Bolpur Brahmacharyashrama".[1] So, Visva-Bharati enjoyed the copyright of literary works as well as musical notation of Rabindranath through its publications unit Granthan Vibhaga and Musical Board in Kolkata up to December 2001. After expiry of copyright private publishers are now free to publish Tagoreana. The present study is an attempt to find out:

- Is the Tagoreana being published simultaneously by large private publishing houses as well as small and new publishers in Bengali?

- What percentage of Tagoreana is being published by private publishers?
- Are the Visva-Bharati publications more costly?
- What will be the fate of less popular/commercially non-viable writings of Tagoreana?

Pre-Visva-Bharati Publication of Tagoreana

The first book of Rabindranath *Kavi-Kahini* was published in the year 1878 by his friend Prabodh Chandra Ghosh. Regarding this publication Rabindranath wrote "When I was in Ahmedabad with my brother, my friend astonished me by sending this book."[2] The second one *Banaphul* was published in the year 1880 by the poet's elder brother Somendranath. Sailesh Chandra Majumdar of Majumdar Library was the first professional publisher who first published *Kavyagrantha* (collected works) of Rabindranath in the year 1903-04. Before that Rabindranath had to publish his works using his own fund with the exception of *Kadi o Komal* (published in 1886 by People's Library), *Chithipatra* (published in 1887 by Saratkumar Lahiri & Co.), and *Panchabhut* (published in 1897 by Sur Company). Books published from Adi Brahmasamaja Jantra were exclusively funded from his own fund given by his father Debendranath Tagore. Sometimes Rabindranath had to face serious scarcity of funds for publication as well as to meet the expenses of Santiniketan Ashrama. Tagoreana was even sold in half price from bookshops like Sri Sri Chaitanya Pustakalaya, 9 Cornwallis Street, Kolkata in the year 1304 (B.S.) through press advertisement. Even Rabindranath expressed his willingness to give up copyright of his collected works and publications up to *Kshanika* (1900) for rupees six thousand only to any person in a letter addressed to Priyanath Sen in 1307 (B.S.).[3]

But the situation changed with the establishment of Visva-Bharati Granthan Vibhaga (VBGV), the Publishing Department of the University, as an integral part of Visva-Bharati. It was established by Rabindranath in the year 1923 and published dance drama *Basanta* in the same year. But regular publication started from the year 1925 with the publication of *Puravi.* Before that the publication right of Tagoreana was given to Chintamani Ghosh, owner of Indian Press/Indian Publishing House of Allahabad. In a letter dated 18th September, 1922 Rabindranath wrote "I have given the right of all my Bengali books to Visva-Bharati in a deed and relieved now."[4] According to Tagore's biographer Prabhatkumar "Chintamoni Kar took the responsibility of publishing the poet's publication with the negotiation of Ramananda Chattopadhyaya in 1908. The stock value of 100 books published up to 1923 was Rs. 78,000. Chintamanibabu gave his entire stock to Visva-Bharati at the cost of Rs. 26,000 only."[5]

Visva-Bharati Publication of Tagoreana

Visva-Bharati Granthan Vibhaga (VBGV) started its functioning in the house named *'Mahatashrama'* at Cornwallis Street near Vidyasagar College in Kolkata with the initial capital of Rs. 26,000, taken as loan from central fund of Visva-Bharati which the institute repaid during next nineteen years.[6] The objectives of the department are based on a set of rules laid down by Rabindranath himself:

1. The complete works of Tagore should be available at an affordable cost. (*'Sulabha Rabindranath'*).
2. These should be accurately published in respect of spelling, style, presentation and format. (*'Bisuddha Rabindranath'*)
3. The complete writings of Tagore (*'Samagra Rabindranath'*) should be published.[7]

To fulfil the aforesaid objectives the principal activities of the publishing department includes publication and marketing of books written by Rabindranath, on Rabindranath, on Rabindra associates, disciplines and students, on Visva-Bharati and Santiniketan and also publication of textbooks. At the initial years after the establishment of VBGB Rabindranath was anxious about its success. But, in course of time it was observed that the readers as well as sales of Tagoreana increased day by day as found from following Table 6.1 sales figure:

Table 6.1: Turn-over of VBGV: 1921-22 to 1926-27

Financial Year	*Sale (Rs.)*
1921-22	19,800
1922-23	19,743
1923-24	22,000
1924-25	16,594
1925-26	25,039
1926-27	28,738

Source: Visva-Bharati Granthan Vibhaga: Panchasatvarsha Parikrama.

Prasantachandra Mahalanobis served the institute as its first director. The successive directors were Kishorimohan Santra, Charuchandra Bhattacharya, Pulinbehari Sen. The members of the first publishing committee besides Rabindranath were Surendranath Tagore, Ramananda Chattopadhyay, Tapanmohan Chattopadhyay, Nepalchandra Ray, Rathindranath Tagore and Prasantachandra Mahalanobis. Right from the beginning Prasantachandra started to provide detailed information about a book of Rabindranath published by VBGV under the heading *"Patha-parichaya"* and included it either at the beginning or at the end of a book. Later on *"Patha-parichaya"* termed as *"Granthaparichaya"* and included at the end of the book. *Granthaparichaya* included detail information about the first publication, later editions, criticism, changes in manuscripts, and Rabindranath's comment on his own writings. Later on, it was also included in *Rabindra-Rachanavali* by Prasantachandra. The same process was followed and further developed by the successive directors. Thus, VBGV is the pioneer publisher of Bengali book world with special research-based information. The institute published not only collected works on special themes, but also publications of new editions with collection from different editions of the same book. As a result the institute was able to establish itself as a centre for Tagoreana culture and research.[8] For maintaining spelling and pronouncing standard uniformly for all publications of Tagoreana Prasantachandra took special care obviously in consultation with Rabindranath. Sunitikumar Chattopadhyay and Kalidas Nag also helped him in this respect.[9] Thus, VBGV from its very beginning tried to be one of the best publishing houses as well as centre for Rabindra culture with its printing and editorial quality, uniform spelling throughout all the publications as well as house style to fulfil Tagore's vision of *Samagra Rabindranath* and *Bisuddha Rabindranath*. The intellectual reader community accepted it which can be established from the sales figures recorded in Table 6.2.

Sales figures significantly increased in the financial year 1961-62 as 1961 was celebrated as Rabindranath's centenary year throughout the country. Though VBGV started its career with publications of Tagoreana in the year 1923, but from the year 1942 it started to publish books on Rabindranath, Rabindra associates, Visva-Bharati, and Santiniketan as well. Meanwhile VBGV started publishing *Rabindra Rachanavali* (Collected Works of Rabindranath) from the year 1939

Table 6.2: Turnover of VBGV: 1960-61 to 1964-65

Financial Year	*Sale (Rs.)*
1960-61	13,85,288
1961-62	18,17,637
1962-63	14,64,007
1963-64	14,26,699
1964-65	15,40,755

Source: Visva-Bharati Granthan Vibhaga: Panchasatvarsha Parikrama.

under the directorship of Charuchandra Bhattacharya.[10] Visva-Bharati became the Central University and declared as a Centre of National Importance by the Parliament of India in the year 1952; from then the activities of VBGV became more formal.

VBGV is rendering its services continuously for nearly seven decades. Rabindranath's intention was not only to see his works published properly and to keep these in print, but also to provide constant financial support to the parent organization out of the income generated by the department. The department remained a self-sufficient unit of Visva-Bharati until the last decade. At present there are 864 titles at the disposal of VBGV. It includes 334 titles by Rabindranath, 174 titles on Rabindranath and 356 other books. It also distributes Visva-Bharati research publications and journals. The publishing department published 19 text books for West Bengal Board of Higher Secondary Education besides 21 school text books written by Rabindranath.[11]

VBGV distributes its publications through a network of distributors for distributing its publications in India, Bangladesh and other foreign countries through its head office (6, Acharya Jagadish Chandra Bose Road, Kolkata-17), two sales counters at Kolkata (2, Bankim Chatterjee Street, Kolkata-73 and 210, Bidhan Sarani, Kolkata-6) and one in Santiniketan (inaugurated in August 2003). In the year 2013-14 there were 23 agents for distributing Visva-Bharati Publication in India and abroad. For sales promotion activity VBGV regularly participates in different book fairs and exhibitions in Kolkata, as well as in national, state, district book fairs and exhibitions. For example in the year 2014-15 the institute participated in 14 book fair including world book fair at New Delhi and two state book fairs at Guwahati (Assam) and Agartala (Tripura). In every year the publishing unit publishes new books. In the year 2014-15, 56 books published which includes new books, new edition and books written by Rabindranath reprinted.[12]

After the expiry of copyright there was an impression that all the leading as well as other relatively small private publishers will start publishing Tagoreana and turnover of Visva-Bharati Publications will reduce significantly. The following turnover Table may unveil the truth:

Table 6.3: Turnover of VBGV (1997-2006)

Financial Year	*Sale (Rs.)*
1997-98	2,18,35,671.00
1998-99	2,10,92,814.00
1999-00	2,28,69,990.00
2000-01	2,50,81,547.00
2001-02	2,20,04,541.00
2002-03	2,30,92,791.00
2003-04	2,01,75,016.00
2004-05	1,69,02,235.00
2005-06	6,39,88,728.00
2006-07	6,98,82,018.00

Source: Visva-Bharati Annual Report and Annual Audited Account.

It reveals from Table 6.3 that sales are steady and increasing except years 2004-05. But in later years sales reduced remarkably. One of the main reason is that Government of West Bengal withdraw the procurement order of school text books like Sahaj Path from Granthan Vibhaga. Even sales reduced to Rs. 15 lakhs only in the financial year 2010-11. So after lapses of copyright of Tagore's work, it became difficult for VBGV to maintain level of accuracy of the text and continually update existing volumes with new research. To save Visva-Bharati Publishing Department Ministry of Human Resource Development, Government of India and University Grants Commission (UGC) have taken the responsibility of 31 sanctioned posts in Visva-Bharati and making final move towards integration of the unit with Visva-Bharati with effect from 2009. From 2007-08 UGC started sanctioning financial grant as a result VBGV received Rs. 10 lakhs from unassigned grant scheme of UGC in 2007-08. Sales turnover again slowly increases and reached to Rs. 1,43,80,216 in the financial year 2013-14. It is an indication that intellectual community till considers Visva-Bharati Publication as standard.

Publication of Tagoreana by Private Publishers after the Expiry of Copyright

After the expiry of copyright in December 2001 Tagoreana is open and private publishers are free to publish Tagoreana. The following Table 6.4 gives some idea about total number of publishers publishing Tagoreana.

Table 6.4: Publishers of Bengali Books (2002-2006)

Sl. No.	*Year*	*No. of Publishers Publishing Bengali Books*	*No. of Publishers Publishing Tagoreana*	*% of Publishers Publishing Tagoreana*
1.	2002	688	12	1.74
2.	2003	688	12	1.74
3.	2004	755	32	4.24
4.	2005	755	38	5.03
5.	2006	658	38	5.76

Source: Books in Print from West Bengal and Fair Directory 2002-2006.

From Table 6.4 it is evident that only a meagre percentage of publishers are publishing Tagoreana even five years after the expiry of copyright. Moreover, names of many publishers like Ranar, Nandita, Saroj etc. are in the Books in Print, but books are not available in the market and many publishers publish only one or two books like *Sahaj Path*. Thus, for this study twenty-five publishers were considered. The descending order of first fourteen publishers in respect of number of publication are: Kamini Prakashalaya (45), Juthika Book Stall (18), United Publishers (15), Patraj Publication (15), Punascha (11), Ashok Book Agency (10), Granthasambhar (9), Sahityam (7), Gitanjali (6), Tuli-Kalam (6), Patra Bharati (6), Nirmal Book Agency (5), Asia Publishing Company (5), Narayan Pustakalaya (4).

A comparative study of the above publications with Visva-Bharati publications reveals that only 39 titles are published by private publishers after the expiry of copyright in comparison of 334 titles of VBGV. Even if English publications, translations into other languages and textbooks of Visva-Bharati are excluded, the ratio would be 282:39. The number of publications of private publishers excludes selective publications from short stories which are part of *Galpaguchchha* (Collection of short stories) published by VBGV. Actually most of the publishers published books with the titles of one or two short stories like *Khoka Babur Partyabartan, Cabuliwala, Postmaster* etc. selecting from *Galpaguchchha*. Another important feature may be observed that most of the publishers published *Gitanjali, Sanchayita, Gitabitan* and *Galpaguchchha*. The remaining books are mostly novels, one or two dramas and autobiography of Rabindranath. But books on songs, dramas, essays, religious writings, travel, education, rural development and *Rabindra Rachanavali* are not yet published by private publishers. Publishers getting their books printed from many printers indicate that most of them have no in-house printing press. Leading publishers of Bengali books like Ananda Publishers, Dey's Publishing, Sahityaloke have not yet started publishing Tagoreana and Mitra & Ghosh published only four books. Relatively new publishers with less number of titles in their credit as observed from their current catalogue like Juthika Book Stall (105 titles), United Publishers (147 titles), Ashok Book Agency (138 titles), *Granthasambhar* (53 titles), *Gitanjali* (79 titles), Asia Publishing Company (107 titles), Radha Pustakalaya (144 titles) etc. started publishing Tagoreana who generally publish children's books, classics and books of authors whose copyright expired like Rabindranath Tagore, Saratchandra Chattopadhyay, Bankim Chandra Chattopadhyay, Sukumar Ray, and Dakshinaranjan Ray.

Comparison of Price of Tagoreana Published by Visva-Bharati and Private Publishers

For marketing of books, besides sales channel, discount structure, advertisement etc. price plays a vital role. It is more important after the expiry of copyright as no monopoly of Visva-Bharati exists now. Table 6.5 will help to have an idea about comparative price of titles, as discount structure of all the publishers are almost the same, i.e. 33.3 per cent to booksellers.

It is evident from Table 6.5 that the price of most of the titles of VBGV is higher than any other private publishers though all the titles of Visva-Bharati in the comparative table are paperback except *Sanchayita, Gitabitan, Galpaguchchha* and *Sey*. Books published by private publishers are hardbound (except four titles of *Sahityam, Gitanjali, Sesher Kavita, Sisu* and *Sisu Bholanath*, two titles of Prakash Bhavana: *Jivansmriti* and *Chhelebela*, one title each of Bak-Sahitya: *Rajarshi*, Suranjana Prakashani: *Sesher Kavita* and *Sahaj Path* of Babli, Mitra & Ghosh and Patra Bharati), but the binding quality is poor in general except books published by Mitra & Ghosh. It appears that the price of *Dui Bon* published by Kamini Prakashalaya is much higher (Rs. 25.00) than Visva-Bharati (Rs. 12.00), but *Dui Bon* published by Kamini included four other short

Table 6.5: Comparative Statement of Price: VBGV and Private Publishers

Part I

Title	*VBGV*	Kamini	*Juthika*	*United*	*Patraj*	*Punascha*	*Ashok*	*Granthas-ambhar*
Gitanjali	50.00	40.00	30.00	40.00	40.00	35.00	25.00	45.00
Sanchayita	160.00	100.00	100.00		110.00	90.00	130.00	120.00
Gitabitan	325.00	100.00	120.00		120.00	90.00	150.00	
Galpaguchchha	225.00	110.00	120.00		120.00	110.00	110.00	
Ghare-Baire	70.00	40.00		30.00	50.00	35.00		50.00
Naukadubi	70.00	50.00	50.00	45.00	60.00	45.00	65.00	60.00
Chaturanga	35.00	25.00		25.00	25.00	38.00		
Char Adhyay	35.00	25.00	40.00	25.00	30.00	25.00		
Bau-Thakuranir Hat	60.00	30.00	30.00	30.00	35.00	25.00		
Rajarshi	40.00	30.00	40.00	25.00	35.00	25.00		
Dui Bon	12.00	25.00		25.00	30.00			
Chokher Bali	65.00	50.00	50.00		40.00		55.00	50.00
Malancha	13.00	25.00		25.00	20.00			50.00
Yogayog	40.00	50.00	40.00	40.00	60.00		45.00	50.00
Gora	130.00	80.00		70.00		60.00		80.00
Sesher Kavita	45.00	30.00	40.00					
Dakghar	20.00	30.00						
Raktakarabi	25.00	25.00	35.00					
Sisu	45.00	25.00		35.00				
Sisu Bholanath	25.00	25.00		30.00				
Chandalika	8.00	30.00						
Chitrangada	35.00	30.00		30.00				
Raja o Rani	55.00	30.00						
Tin-Sangi	40.00	30.00						
Chhinnapatra	100.00	40.00	45.00					45.00
Katha o Kahini	40.00	25.00						
Visarjan	25.00	25.00	30.00					
Sonar Tari	35.00	40.00	40.00				45.00	
Jivansmriti	40.00	50.00	40.00				45.00	
Natir Puja	20.00	30.00						
Punascha	60.00	30.00					45.00	
Chitra	40.00		40.00					
Lipika	60.00		22.00					

Part II

Title	*VBGV*	*Sahityan*	*Gitanjali*	*Tuli-Kalam*	*Patra Bharati*	*Nirmal Book*	*Asia Pub*	*Narayan*
Gitanjali	50.00	16.00		30.00			60.00	45.00
Sanchayita	160.00	80.00		80.00			125.00	120.00
Gitabitan	325.00	100.00		100.00			150.00	130.00
Galpaguchchha	225.00	100.00		80.00			150.00	130.00

(Contd.)

Title	VBGV	Sahityan	Gitanjali	Tuli-Kalam	Patra Bharati	Nirmal Book	Asia Pub	Narayan
Ghare-Baire	70.00				40.00			
Chaturanga	35.00				15.00			
Char Adhyay	35.00				15.00			
Malancha	13.00				15.00			
Sesher Kavita	45.00	20.00	30.00		25.00			
Sisu	45.00	20.00	30.00					
Sisu Bholanath	25.00	15.00	25.00					
Chhinnapatra	100.00		40.00					
Chhelebala	20.00		25.00	20.00		25.00		
Khapchhada	225.00					60.00		

Source: Publisher Catalogue.

stories namely *Sampatti Samarpan, Khoka Babur Pratyabartan, Thakurda* and *Taraprasannar Kriti.* Similarly, along with *Malancha* two other short stories *Guptadhan* and *Kankal* are included. *Dakghar* is a combination of three dramas *Dakghar, Malini* and *Mukut. Chandalika* is a combination of two dramas—*Chandalika* and *Tapati. Natir Puja* and *Arupratan* are combined together under one cover. The price of *Gitanjali*—bilingual edition of Asia Publishing seems to be higher but the price of the same edition of Visva-Bharati is much higher, i.e. Rs. 125.00. *Jivansmriti* published by Mitra & Ghosh is an edited volume by Baridbaran Ghosh with good numbers of notes and references and contains more pages (N = 352) than that of VBGB (N = 163). *Sahaj Path* published by Patra Bharati and Babli contains exercise with more number of pages.

In this comparative price statement titles not published by VBGV as a separate book was not considered. For that reason *Karuna* published by Patraj, books separately published by the name of short stories, titles made on selective writings like *Chhotodar Lekha of Asia* or *Kishor Rabindranath* of Mitra & Ghosh are not considered.

Comparison of Page and Size of Tagoreana Published by Visva-Bharati and Private Publishers

Price is related to number of pages, size of the book, paper and printing quality, illustrations etc. So, a comparative statement of pages along with size of the book may throw some light on the above aspect of comparative price statement.

Table 6.6: Comparative Statement of Page and Size: VBGV and Private Publishers

Part I

Title	*VBGV*	*Kamini*	*Juthika*	*United*	*Patraj*	*Punascha*	*Ashok*	*Grantha-sambhar*
Gitanjali	194	152	104	152	128	176	128	152
	18X12	21.7X13.7	22X13.5	21.7X13.5	22X14	21.8X14	21.7X13.6	21.7X14
Sanchayita	918	736	606		607	575	664	720
	21.8X14.5	21.7X13.7	22X14		21.5X14	21.8 X14	21.9X13.7	21.7X13.8
Gitabitan	1034	784	764		706	660	784	
	21.8X14.5	21.7X13.7	22X14		22.3X14	21.8X14	22.3X14.2	
Galpaguchchha	882	848	768		848	672	879	
	21.5X14.5	21.7X13.7	22X14		22X14	21.8X14.5	22.1X14.2	
Ghare-Baire	220	136		136	160	96		136
	21.3X13.8	13.7X21.7		21.7X13.5	22X14	21.8X14		21.5X14
Naukadubi	279	176	176	176	208	134	208	176
	21.5X14	21.7X13.7	21.5X13.7	21.7X13.5	22X14	21.11X14	21.7X14	21.5X14
Chaturanga	117	64		64	72	144		
	18.3X12.3	21.7X13.7		21.7X13.5	22X14	21.10X14		
Char Adhyay	116	80	40	64	71	62		
	18.5X12.5	21.7 X 13.7	21.7X13.5	21.7X13.5	21.7X13.8	21.10X14		
Bau-Thakuranir Hat	208	104	96	104	120	78		
	18X12	21.7X13.7	22X13.6	21.7X13.5	22X14	21.10X14		
Rajarshi	175	96	88	96	112	68		
	18X12	21.7X13.7	22X13.5	21.7X13.5	22.2X13.9	22X14		
Dui Bon	103	80		64	61			
	17.6X12	21.7X13.7		21.7X13.5	22X14			
Chokher Bali	242	160	152		167		168	160
	21.6X13.7	21.7X13.7	21.5X13.5		22X14		21.7X14	2 .5X14
Malancha	96	72		48	56			216
	17.8X12.1			21.7X13.5	22X14			2 .5X14
Yogayog	237	144	136	144	19122X14		160	144
	21.4X13.9		22X13.7	21.7X13.5			22X13.7	2 .5X14
Gora	503	288		288		228		288
	21.6X14			21.7X13.5		22X14		2 .5X14
Sesher Kavita	190	96	72					
	17.9X12		22X13.7					
Dakghar	79	96						
	17.8x12							
Raktakarabi	123	80	72					
	21.5x13.5		21.8X14					
Sisu	204	72		112				
	17.5x12			21.7X13.5				
Sisu Bholanath	90	64		64				
	18x12.2			21.7X13.5				
Chandalika	47	96						
	18x12							
Chitrangada	61	96						
	20.8x13.1							
Raja o Rani	159	96						
	18x12							
Tin-Sangi	126	88						
	21.3x14							
Chhinnapatra	311	128	120	126				128
	21.5x13.6		22X13.9	21.7X13.5				21.5X14

(*Contd.*)

Title	*VBGV*	*Kamini*	*Juthika*	*United*	*Patraj*	*Punascha*	*Ashok*	*Grantha-sambhar*
Katha o Kahini	171 18x12.2	80						
Visarjan	128 18.12.2	80	70 21.5X13.5					
Sonar Tari	177 18x12	128	120 22X13.7				144 22X13.7	
Jivansmriti	163 21.2x13.5	160	114 21.4X13.9				128 21.8X13.8	
Natir Puja	88 18x12	96						
Punascha	217 21.5x13.8	104					128 21.8X13.8	
Chitra	175 17.5x12		127 22X13.3					
Lipika	180 18x12		72 21.5X13.5					

Part II

Title	*VBGV*	*Sahityan*	*Gitanjali*	*Tuli-Kalam*	*Patra Bharati*	*Nirmal Book*	*Asia Publishing*	*Narayan*
Gitanjali	194 18X12	151 17.5X12.2		192 21.5X13.5			239 19X10.5	176 21.7X14
Sanchayita	918 21.8X14.5	632 22X14.3		780 22X14			640 21.7X14	722 22X13.8
Gitabitan	1034 21.8X14.5	783 22X14.5		959 22X14			824 22X14	764 21.8X14
Galpaguchchha	882 21.5X14.5	896 22X14.5		800 22X14			904 22X14	848 22X13.8
Ghare-Baire	220 21.3X13.8				250 17.7X11.4			
Chaturanga	117 18.3X12.3				96 17.9X11.2			
Char Adhyay	116 18.5X12.5				96 17.8X11.4			
Malancha	96 17.8X12.1				95 17.8X11.4			
Sesher Kavita	190 17.9X12	128 18X12.3	96 21.5X13.7		144 18X11.5			
Sisu	204 17.5x12	175 18X12	96 21.5X13.5					
Sisu Bholanath	90 18x12.2	80 18X12	64 21.5X13.5					
Chhinnapatra	311 21.5x13.6		120 21.5X13.5					
Chhelebela	83 18X12.4		64 21.5X13.5	72 22X13.8		64 24.5X18.5		
Khapchhada	160.00 25X19.5					159 24.5X19		

From Table 6.6, it is clear that the number oTf pages of the books published by VBGV is much higher in many cases nearly twice in comparison to the number of pages of books published by private publishers through the size remains more or less same. In some cases like *Malancha* of Granthasambhar it may be noticed that the number of pages is higher, but it is a combination of four novels, namely *Malancha, Dui Bon, Char Adhyay* and *Chaturanga.* The actual page of *Malancha* is 48 only. Thus, it is evident that to keep price low, the private publishers compromised on paper, binding and printing quality, font size, space between lines and also top and bottom margins which in many cases violate aesthetic beauty and also publishing quality.

Growth of Publication of Tagoreana by Private Publishers

Copyright of Tagoreana expired in December 2001. Publishers started publishing Tagoreana from January 2002. A brief statement

Table 6.7: Year of first Publication of Tagoreana by Private Publishers.

Publishers	*2002*	*2003*	*2004*	*2005*	*2006*	*Total*
Kamini	39	6				45
Juthika	18					18
United	15					15
Patraj	15					15
Punascha	11					11
Ashok	8	2				10
Grantha sambhar	9					9
Sahityam	4	2	1			7
Gitanjali	4			1		6
Tuli-Kalam	5			1		6
Patra Bharati	4	2				6
Nirmal	1	4				5
Asia	5					5
Narayan	4					4
Mitra & Ghosh		3			1	4
Radha					3	3
Reflect	3					3
Das Sahitya Kutir	2	1				3
Book Front	3					3
Prakash Bhavana						2
Sahitya Bharati						2
Babli	1					1
Bak Sahitya		1				1
Rajarshi			1			1
Suranjana		1				1

of first publication of Tagoreana by various private publishers will indicate the growth of publication as well as flow of business interest of private publishers in publishing Tagoreana after the expiry of copyright.

From Table 6.7, it is clear that 81 per cent (151 out of 186) books published in the year 2002 immediately after the expiry of copyright. Nearly 13 per cent (22 out of 186) books (new titles not published in 2002) were published in the year 2003. So, remaining 6 per cent books published in the last three years (2004-06). Moreover, most of the books published in 2002 were in between January and May 2002. The year of publication has not been mentioned in case of *Sesher Kavita* published by *Gitanjali* and two titles each of Prakash Bhavana and Sahitya Bharati entitled *Sisu Bholanath* and *Jivansmriti* and *Sahaj path* parts I and II respectively. Thus, majority of publishers published books in a hurry immediately after the expiry of copyright which increased the possibility of mistakes.

International Standard Book Number (ISBN) allotted by Raja Rammohun Roy Library Foundation, Calcutta is an important tool for bibliographic control. Tagoreana published by Visva-Bharati incorporated it. So, a study of Tagoreana published after the expiry of copyright by private publishers with ISBN may reveal the real situation in this respect.

It is clear that five publishers (Patraj, Punascha, Mitra & Ghosh, Reflect and Book Front) published Tagoreana with ISBN. In other words, five publishers out of twenty-five (i.e. 20%) published Tagoreana with ISBN. If titles having ISBN is considered, the figure would be 36 out of 186 titles, i.e. 19 per cent only. It indicates less bibliographical control over publication of Tagoreana after expiry of copyright.

Regarding copyright declarations only three publishers (Grantha sambhar, Mitra & Ghosh, and Reflect) had clearly mentioned that they reserved the copyright. Five publishers (Kamini, Punascha, Sahityayan, Juthika and United) mentioned the title as the publisher's first edition, but without any sign of copyright. The remaining 17 publishers are silent regarding copyright issue.

Discussion

It was observed during the study that though most of the books published by private publishers are hardbound, the binding as well as paper and printing quality in general is poor except the publication of Mitra & Ghosh. Regarding design of cover page Visva-Bharati follows a house style of saffron cover (with such exceptions as *Raktakarabi, Chhinnapatra, Natir puja, Khapchhada, Chandalika* and *Sey*) which is the symbol of sacrifice with title and signature of Rabindranath Tagore in front cover in brown or red and Visva-Bharati logo, price and ISBN at the back cover. Out of 186 titles compared for this study, cover pages of 64 books contain photograph of Rabindranath, 21 contain paintings and drawings of Rabindranath, and theme of the story is drawn in 89 titles and 12 titles with theme and Rabindranath's photo both. The cover page with theme is mostly scene of cinematography of Rabindranath's popular novels.

In case of Tagoreana published by Visva-Bharati, either there is an introduction by Rabindranath Tagore himself (with the exception in *Gitanjali* where the introduction is by W.B. Yeats) or without any introduction. For example, out of 41 titles compared for this study, on 14 occasions Rabindranath wrote the introduction. In most of the cases books published by private publishers included the introduction of Rabindranath whenever available and at the same time introduction written by some others also included. It is interesting to note that Sudeb Mukhopadhyay (no official address given) wrote introductions for three publishers: Kamini Prakashalaya (in 14 books), United Publisher (in 2 books) and Granthasambhar (in 2 books). The same introduction was used thrice in *Gitanjali* published by three publishers, twice in *Chhinnapatra* published by Kamini Prakashalaya and Granthasambhar and twice in *Rajarshi* published by Kamini Prakashalaya and United Publisher. As most of the introducers did not give their official or residential addresses questions are likely be raised about the authenticity and also academic credibility to introduce Tagoreana.

In a good number of books published by Visva-Bharati, *Granthaparichaya* has tremendous research value as it provides information regarding first publication, change in manuscript by Rabindranath, criticism, Rabindranath's own interpretation etc. Out of 41 titles of Visva-Bharati compared, 23 have this kind of

Granthaparichaya. Most of the private publications of Tagoreana lack this kind of *Granthaparichaya* though publishers like Patraj in *Sanchayita* and *Gitabitan* and Ashok Book Agency in *Sonar Tari* and *Punascha*, Patra Bharati in *Ghare-Baire*, included *Granthaparichaya* of Visva-Bharati. It is worthy to note here that this *Granthaparichaya* section was not written by Rabindranath, in later period it was added with the book by VBGB, first initiated by Charuchandra Bhattacharya. So copying of *Granthaparichaya* is a clear violation of copyright. Only in ten books (two of Kamini—*Gitanjali* and *Gitabitan;* three of Tuli—Kalam-*Gitabitan, Galpaguchchha, Lipika;* four of Patrabharati—*Sesher Kavita, Malancha, Chaturanga, Char Adhyay*; one of Nirmal Book agency—*Khapchhada) Granthaparichaya* has been added as publishers own contribution, but a large portion of it is copied from Visva-Bharati *Granthaparichaya*. In two books published by Mitra & Ghosh *Jivansmriti* and edited by Baridbaran Ghosh; and *Kishor Rabindra Rachanavali* edited by Amitrasudan Bhattacharya provided sufficient notes and references.

Conclusion

Most of the private publishers published Tagoreana with low price which resulted in poor quality in respect of binding, paper and printing quality, small space and font size. As most of the private publishers published Tagoreana immediately after expiry of copyright in a hurry there is scope for further textual comparative study in respect of punctuation-mark mistakes, spelling mistakes, line/word omission /addition, and paragraph clubbed/ separated. A very small portion of commercially viable titles of Tagoreana has been published by private publishers even five years after the expiry of copyright. Tagore's writings on education, religion, nationalism, rural reconstruction, letters etc. have not yet been published by private publishers. Thus, though Tagoreana is now available easily at less cost but '*Bisuddha Rabindranath*' as well as '*Samagra Rabindranath*' is still a distant dream.

References

1. Tagore, Rabindranath (1907), *Vichitra Prabandha*. Calcutta: Visva-Bharati Granthan Vibhaga, p. 149.

Comparison of Page and Size of Tagoreana published by Visva-Bharati and Private Publishers

Price is related to number of pages, size of the book, paper and printing quality, illustrations etc. So, a comparative statement of pages along with size of the book may throw some light on the above aspect of comparative price statement.

Table 7.2: Comparative Statement of Page and Size (in cm): VBGV and Private Publishers

Title	*VBGV*	*Kamini*	*Juthika*	*United*	*Patraj*	*Punascha*
Ghare-Baire	220	136		136	160	96
	21.3X13.8	13.7X21.7		21.7X13.5	22X14	21.8X14
Naukadubi	279	176	176	176	208	134
	21.5X14	21.7X13.7	21.5X13.7	21.7X13.5	22X14	21.11X14
Chaturanga	117	64		64	72	144
	18.3X12.3	21.7X13.7		21.7X13.5	22X14	21.10X14
Char Adhyay	116	80	40	64	71	62
	18.5X12.5	21.7 X 13.7	21.7X13.5	21.7X13.5	21.7X13.8	21.10X14
Bau-Thakuranir	208	104	96	104	120	78
Hat	18X12	21.7X13.7	22X13.6	21.7X13.5	22X14	21.10X14
Rajarshi	175	96	88	96	112	68
	18X12	21.7X13.7	22X13.5	21.7X13.5	22.2X13.9	22X14
Dui Bon	103	80		64	61	
	17.6X12	21.7X13.7		21.7X13.5	22X14	
Chokher Bali	242	160	152		167	
	21.6X13.7	21.7X13.7	21.5X13.5		22X14	
Malancha	96	72		48	56	
	17.8X12.1			21.7X13.5	22X14	
Yogayoga	237	144	136	144	19122X14	
	21.4X13.9		22X13.7	21.7X13.5		
Gora	503	288		288		228
	21.6X14			21.7X13.5		22X14
Sesher Kavita	190	96	72			
	17.9X12		22X13.7			

Source: Book published by different Publishers.

From Table 7.2 it is clear that the number of pages of the books published by VBGV is much higher in many cases nearly twice in comparison to the number of pages of books published by private publishers through the size remains more or less same. Thus, it is evident that to keep price low, the private publishers compromised on paper, binding and printing quality, font size, space between lines and also top and bottom margins which in many cases violate aesthetic beauty and also publishing quality.

Textual Comparison of Tagoreana Published by Private Publishers and Visva-Bharati

A publisher-wise comparative study of titles with Visva-Bharati Publications in respect of mistakes in punctuation marks, spelling, omission of word(s) or line(s), style of presentation etc. would focus on the truth that after the expiry of copyright whether '*Bisuddha Rabindranath*' is being published or not.

In the first literary comparison Table 7.3, punctuation marks changed or omitted in the books published by private publishers from that of Visva-Bharati edition have been compared. Similarly, Table 7.3a shows additional punctuation marks used in the text. Table 7.3b spelling mistakes, omission or addition of word(s) or line(s), paragraph/line clubbed/separated are considered.

Table 7.3: Kamini Prakashalaya: Punctuation Marks Changed or Omitted

Titles	*Page No. Compared*	.	,	:	;	?	!	“ ” ‘ ’	,	—	-	*Total*
Ghare-Baire	14	48	44		14	3	19		3	33	23	187
Naukadubi	18	2	7		1	2	3				3	18
Chaturanga	6	10	4		6			39		4	3	66
Char Adhyay	8	7	5		1		2				6	21
Bau-Thakuranir Hat	10	3	6		1	1	1				3	15
Rajarshi	10	1	20		6	8	5			4	2	46
Dui Bon	8	1	8	1	1		2	2			3	18
Chokher Bali	16	7	17		9	1	6	1		1	16	59
Malancha	7	1	11			13	3				4	32
Yogayoga	14	7	14		3	2	4	1		2	12	45
Gora	29	30	95		30	11	31	15	1	44	18	275
Sesher Kavita	10	4	14		6	11		7	1	5	10	58

Source: Books Published by Kamini Prakashalaya.

Ghare-Baire, Chaturanga and *Gora* are having the highest mistakes—13, 11 and 9 per page respectively in respect of punctuation marks changed or punctuation marks omitted. In *Chandilika, Rajarshi* and *Gora* maximum number of additional punctuation marks—5, 1.5 and 1 respectively per page are used. In case of other mistakes *Sesher Kavita* 9 spelling mistakes in 10 pages. Paragraphs have been clubbed in *Chokher Bali* as many as 19 times in 16 pages compared. It is done mainly to reduce the number of pages to keep price relatively low.

From Tables 7.3a and 7.3b it may be concluded that the highest number of changes or omissions of punctuation marks has been

Table 7.3a: Kamini Prakashalaya: Additional Punctuation Marks Used

Titles	*Page No. Compared*	,	;	:	?	!	“ ” ‘ ’	’	___	-	*Total*
Ghare-Baire	14	2						1			3
Naukadubi	18	3								4	7
Chaturanga	6										0
Char Adhyay	8									6	6
Bau-Thakuranir Hat	10										0
Rajarshi	10	12								3	15
Dui Bon	8									2	2
Chokher Bali	16	9								4	13
Malancha	7	1								3	4
Yogayoga	14	5								5	10
Gora	29	15					1			11	27
Sesher Kavita	10	3								3	6

Source: Books Published by Kamini Prakashalaya.

Table: 7.3b: Kamini Prakashalaya: Other Mistakes

Title	*Page Compared*	*Spelling Mistake*	*Sentence Omitted*	*Word Omitted*	*Sentence Added*	*Word Added*	*Para Clubbed*	*Para Separated*
Ghare-Baire	14	7	1				2	
Naukadubi	18	5						2
Chaturanga	6	1						
Char Adhyay	8	4					1	
Bau-Thakuranir Hat	10	1						
Rajarshi	10	4					4	2
Dui Bon	8	5					5	1
Chokher Bali	16	6		1			19	
Malancha	7	4					4	1
Yogayoga	14	10		1				
Gora	29	12					5	
Sesher Kavita	10	9					4	

Source: Books Published by Kamini Prakashalaya.

made in *Ghare-Baire* (15.14 per page). Similarly, maximum numbers of punctuation marks are added in *Char Adhyaya* (2.14 per page). Maximum spelling mistakes have been noticed in *Dui-Bon* (1 per page), words omitted in *Malancha* (2 words in 5 page), sentences added in *Bau Thakuranir Hat*, words added in *Dui Bon*, paragraphs clubbed in *Malancha* (3 times in 5 pages), paragraphs separated in *Rajarshi* (5 times in 10 pages). During the study some other omissions/mistakes were observed such as: quote omitted in the entire text of *Chaturanga*. Rabindranath dedicated *Bau Thakuranir Hat* to Soudamini Devi through a poem of 24 lines and *Dui Bon* to

Table: 7.4: United Publishers: Punctuation Marks Changed or Omitted

Titles	*Page No. Compared*	.	,	:	;	?	!	“ ” ‘ ’	’	—	-	*Total*
Ghare-Baire	14	51	56		14	5	23			39	24	212
Naukadubi	17	4	14		3	6	3	2			10	42
Chaturanga	6	15	11		5			36		9	1	77
Char Adhyay	7	18	8				2		1	1	6	36
Bau-Thakuranir Hat	10	4	12		2	4	6			2	2	32
Rajarshi	10	4	18		8	3	7		1	6	5	52
Dui Bon	7	6	12		4		1	2		1	3	29
Malancha	5	6	13		3	15	3			3	1	44
Yogayoga	14	8	20		3	3	4	2		15	1	56
Gora	27	33	100		23	4	16	16		36	35	263

Source: Books Published by United Publishers.

Table 7.4a: United Publishers: Additional Punctuation Marks Used

Titles	*Page No. Compared*	.	,	:	;	?	!	“ ” ‘ ’	’	—	-	*Total*
Ghare-Baire	14	1	8				1		6	1	12	29
Naukadubi	17		6						2		8	16
Chaturanga	6											0
Char Adhyay	7		4								11	15
Bau-Thakuranir Hat	10		2								4	6
Rajarshi	10		7							2	1	10
Dui Bon	7		4								4	8
Malancha	5		5						1	2	2	10
Yogayoga	14		5						1		10	16
Gora	27		29		1				1		18	49

Source: Books Published by United Publishers.

Table 7.4b: United Publishers: Other Mistakes

Titles	*Page Compared*	*Spelling Mistake*	*Sentence Omitted*	*Word Omitted*	*Sentence Added*	*Word Added*	*Para Clubbed*	*Para Separated*
Ghare-Baire	14	9	1				1	5
Naukadubi	17	7		2			1	1
Chaturanga	6	1						
Char Adhyay	7	4						
Bau-Thakuranir Hat	10	6			1			
Rajarshi	10	1				1	3	5
Dui Bon	7	7		1		1	2	1
Malancha	5	3		2			3	
Yogayoga	14	6		3				
Gora	27	13		1			5	1

Source: Books Published by United Publishers.

Rajsekher Basu, but the publication of United Publishers excludes this dedication.

Table 7.5: Patraj Publications: Punctuation Marks Changed or Omitted

Titles	*Page No. Compared*	.	,	:	;	?	!	“ ” ‘ ’	'	—	-	*Total*
Ghare-Baire	17	16	16		8	3	8	1	1	11	14	78
Naukadubi	21		1								1	2
Chaturanga	7	8	1		2		1	33			4	49
Char Ahhyay	8	1						1				2
Bau Thakuranir Hat	12	2	9		5	3	11	7		2	4	43
Rajarshi	11									1		1
Dui Bon	6											0
Chokher Bali	17	8	10		11		3			2	11	45
Malancha	6	3	5		3	12	21	2	1	1	3	51
Yogayoga	19	2	4			2					1	9

Source: Books Published by Patraj Publications.

Table 7.5a: Patraj Publications: Additional Punctuation Marks Used

Titles	*Page No. Compared*	.	,	:	;	?	!	“ ” ‘ ’	'	—	-	*Total*
Ghare-Baire	17		3								3	6
Naukadubi	21											0
Chaturanga	7											0
Char Adhyay	8											0
Bau Thakuranir Hat	12		4								5	9
Rajarshi	11											0
Dui Bon	6											0
Chokher Bali	17		3								2	5
Malancha	6		4								4	8
Yogayoga	19		2								6	8

Source: Books Published by Patraj Publications.

A quick look into above Table 7.5 would reveal that the highest and lowest number of other punctuation marks changed or omitted are *Chaturanga* (7 per page) and *Dui Bon* (no mistake) respectively. The highest and lowest number of additional punctuation marks have been used in *Malancha* (1.33 per page) and *Naukadubi* (no addition in 21 page compared) respectively.

It may be concluded from Tables (7.6, 7.6a, and 7.6b) that in case punctuation marks or punctuation marks changed or omitted the chronological order of books having higher mistakes would

Table 7.5b: Patraj Publications: Other Mistakes

Titles	Page Compared	Spelling Mistake	Sentence Omitted	Word Omitted	Line Added	Word Added	Para Clubbed	Para Separated
Ghare-Baire	17	4		1			2	1
Naukadubi	21	2	2					
Chaturanga	7	3					1	
CharAdhyay	8	2	1					
Bau Thakuranir Hat	12	3					2	
Rajarshi	11	5	1					
Dui Bon	6	1						
Chokher Bali	17		1		1		6	
Malancha	6	17	1				3	
Yogayoga	19	4						

Source: Books Published by Patraj Publications.

be *Sesher Kavita* (9 per page), *Rajarshi* (8.33 mistakes per page), *Char Adhyaya* (8.25 mistakes per page) and so on. The highest number of additional punctuation marks has been used in *Char Adhyaya* (4.5 per page). One can observe the highest percentage of spelling mistakes in *Char Adhyaya* (2.25 per page), and the highest number of paragraphs clubbed in *Chokher Bali*.

Table 7.6: Juthika Book Stall: Punctuation Marks Changed or Omitted

Titles	Page No. Compared	.	,	:	;	?	!	“ ” ‘ ’	,	—	-	Total
Naukadubi	18	9	15		3	4	5	2			10	48
Char Adhyay	4	14	7		1						11	33
Bau-Thakuranir Hat	10	8	12		2	8	19	2			2	53
Rajarshi	9	9	26		11	12	6	3		3	5	75
Chokher Bali	15	11	29		18		8	2		2	10	80
Yogayoga	14	2	6			1	3	2		1	6	21
Sesher Kavita	7	3	16	1	6	7	2	2	1	15	10	63

Source: Books Published by Juthika Book Stall.

Table 7.6a: Juthika Book Stall: Additional Punctuation Marks Used

Titles	Page No. Compared	.	,	:	;	?	!	“ ” ‘ ’	,	—	-	Total
Naukadubi	18		6						2		8	16
Char Adhyay	4		4								14	18
Bau-Thakuranir Hat	10	1	5						1		5	12
Rajarshi	9		10								11	21
Chokher Bali	15		29								21	50
Yogayoga	14		6						1	1	3	11
Sesher Kavita	7		16						2	1	7	26

Source: Books Published by Juthika Book Stall.

Table 7.6b: Juthika Book Stall:Other Mistakes

Title	Page Compared	Spelling Mistake	Sentence Omitted	Word Omitted	Sentence Added	Word Added	Para Clubbed	Para Separated
Naukadubi	18	10					1	
Char Adhyay	4	9						
Bau-Thakuranir Hat	10	7						
Rajarshi	9	7				1	2	5
Chokher Bali	15	9		1	2		11	
Yogayoga	14	3						1
Sesher Kavita	7	8						

Source: Books Published by Juthika Book Stall.

Table 7.7: Punaschâ: Punctuation Marks Changed or Omitted

Titles	Page No. Compared	.	,	:	;	?	!	“ ” ‘ ’	,	—	-	Total
Gora	23	18	104		31	5	18	17		54	29	276
Ghare-Baire	9	53	50		19	4	19			30	22	197
Naukadubi	14	1	8		1	4	4	1		4	9	32
Chaturanga	14	7	36		13	1	2	11		1	13	84
Char Adhyay	6	14	16		2	13	17	1		7	11	81
Bau-Thakuranir Hat	7	5	8		1	7	4			2	1	28
Rajarshi	7	4	21		9	14	8	1	1	10	12	80

Source: Books Published by Punascha.

Table 7.7a: Punascha: Additional Punctuation Marks Used

Titles	Page No. Compared	.	,	:	;	?	!	“ ” ‘ ’	,	—	-	Total
Gora	23		31					1		2	19	53
Ghare-Baire	9		10						1		15	26
Naukadubi	14		8								8	16
Chaturanga	14		9					1	1	1	6	18
Char Adhyay	6		9							1	8	18
Bau-Thakuranir Hat	7		2								2	4
Rajarshi	7		8								5	13

Source: Books Published by Punascha.

Table 7.7b: Punascha: Other Mistakes

Title	Page Compared	Spelling Mistake	Sentence Omitted	Word Omitted	Sentence Added	Word Added	Para Clubbed	Para Separated
Gora	23	14					1	
Ghare-Baire	9	3		1			1	
Naukadubi	14	8		1		2	2	
Chaturanga	14	2		1			1	
Char Adhyaya	6	3	20					
Bau-Thakuranir Hat	7	6						
Rajarshi	7	6				1	2	6

Source: Books Published by Punascha.

From the comparative (Tables 7.7, 7.7a, 7.7b) of books published by Punascha and Visva-Bharati. In case of punctuation marks changed or omitted and additional marks used *Ghare-Baire* and *Chaturanga* commit the highest number of mistakes—22 per page and 3 per page respectively. The highest number of spelling mistakes occurred in *Char Adhyaya* (.86 per page), words omitted in *Ghare-Baire* (1 in 9 page). In *Char Adhyaya* which is a combination of *Char Adhyaya* and *Malancha* (Visva-Bharati has no such combined publication) 20 sentences (five paragraphs) have been omitted in *Malancha.* Actually, it starts from sixth paragraph. Rabindranath's dedication of *Ghare-Baire* to Pramathanath Chowdhury, but *Punascha* edition excluded it.

Conclusion

Most of the books published by private publishers are hardbound with poor paper, printing and binding quality. The cover page of novels published by private publishers is mostly taken from the scene of cinematography of Rabindranath's popular novels. The main intension is to attract more reader! It is observed in a study that only 20 per cent publishers published Tagoreana with International Bibliographic Number.[5] This is also true in case of Tagorean fiction. Same introduction written by Sudeb Mukhopadhyay (no official address given) used in fiction *Rajarshi* published by two different publishers Kamini Prakashalaya and United Publisher.

Prasanta Chandra Mahalanobis served the Granthan Vibhaga as its first director. He introduced "*Path-parichaya*" on Tagoreana providing details information about the book and included it at the beginning or end of the books. Later on "*Path-parichaya*" renamed as '*Granthaparichaya*" and included at the end of the book. *Granthaparichaya* provided detailed information about a particular book in respect of its first publication, later editions, criticism, changes or corrections in manuscripts, and Rabindranath Tagore's comment on his own writings. As "*Granthaparichaya*" was not written by Rabindranath, in later period it was added with the book by VBGV, first initiated by Charuchandra Bhattacharya. So copying of *Granthaparichaya* is a clear violation of copyright. This is also observed in published Tagorean fiction by private publishers. Only in case of four fictions, namely *Sesher Kavita,*

Malancha, Chaturanga, Char Adhyaya published by Patrabharati. *Granthaparichaya* has been added as publishers own contribution, but a large portion of it is copied from Visva-Bharati *Granthaparichaya*.

VBGV is the pioneering publisher of the Bengali book world with special research-based information. The institute published not only collected works on special themes, but also publications of new editions with collection from different editions of the same book. As a result the institute was able to establish itself as a centre for Tagoreana culture and research.[6] For maintaining spelling and pronouncing standard uniformly for all publications of Tagoreana, Prasanta Chandra took special care in consultation with Rabindranath Tagore. Suniti Kumar Chattopadhyay and Kalidas Nag also helped him in this respect.[7] Thus, Visva-Bharati Granthan Vibhaga from its very beginning tried to be one of the best publishing houses as well as centre for Rabindra culture with its printing and editorial quality, uniform spelling throughout all the publications as well as house style to fulfil Tagore's vision of *Samagra Rabindranath* and *Bisuddha Rabindranath*. Regarding corrections of manuscripts, its publications in journals or book Rabindranath was very careful.[8] But post copyright publications of Tagoreana by private publisher, besides poor quality paper, binding and printing contain a good number of mistakes. Mistakes in any kind of punctuation mark either addition, omission or exchange affects the meaning, metre, mora and rhythm of writings. This is especially true in case of literature. Change of words, sentences, mistakes in spelling are obviously an indication of injustice to the authors.

References

1. Tagore, Rabindranath. (1998), *Jibansmriti*. Calcutta: Visva-Bharati Granthan Vibhaga, p. 161.
2. Das, Anathnath. (2008), Visva-Bharati Granthan Vibhaga. In *Saraswat: A Collection of Profiles of Some Learned Bodies of West Bengal*. Ed. Badu, Arun Kumar. Kolkata: Paschim Bangla Academy, p. 317.
3. Bhattacharyya, Amitrasudan. (2002), *Pathantar chayan: Rabindra upanyasa*. Kolkata: Visva-Bharati Granthan Vibhaga, p. 272.
4. Ghosh, Debkumar. (1987), *Sonar tari: bishay pathantar*. Hoogly: Sahitya O Desh, p. 174.

5. Ray, P.P. (2012), *Tagore in Print: A Comparative Study before and after expiry of Copyright*. New Delhi: Concept Publishing Co. (P.) Ltd., p. 161.
6. *Visva-Bharati Granthan Vibhaga o Charuchandra Bhattacharyya*. Calcutta: Visva-Bharati Granthan Vibhaga, 1984, p. 54.
7. Das, Anathnath. (2008), Visva-Bharati Granthan Vibhaga. In *Saraswat: A Collection of Profiles of Some Learned Bodies of West Bengal*. Ed. Badu, Arun Kumar. Kolkata: Paschim Bangla Academy, p. 317.
8. Bagchi, Sanat Kumar. (1989), *Rabindra Pandulipi: Samiksha o Bislehsan*. Kolkata: Punthi Pustak, p. 335.

8
Paintings and Drawings of Rabindranath Tagore
An Analytical Study

Introduction

Rabindranath started sketching the manuscript of his writings at the time of writing *"Purabi"* in the year 1924 which can be described as the origin of creation of Rabindranath paintings.[1] But according to available date first painting dates back 15 March, 1929. Up to 1940 Rabindranath had painted more than 2000 paintings and drawings.[2] Victoria Ocampo, while she was nursing the poet back to his health in her villa in Buenos Aires in Argentina in 1924, was impressed upon by seeing the radical imagination of sketch and lines in his notebook and encouraged Rabindranath for drawing and paintings. Later she organized an exhibition of Tagore's paintings at Paris.[3]

In 1930 a series of exhibition of Rabindranath's art work were organized in Europe. Reviews in general to the exhibition of 1930 were complementary. Critiques expressed surprise at the unexpected beauty of the works with imagination. But before that Rabindranath was not confident about his paintings. He wrote to William Rothenstein "My pictures certainly possess psychological interest being products of untutored figures and untrained mind. I am sure they do not reveal a strangeness born of my utter inexperience and individual limitations".[4] Rabindranath had no formal training in art besides the cultural ambience of the family. But according to Rabindranath "the only training which I had from my young days was the training in rhythm in thought, the rhythm in sound. I had come to know that rhythm gives reality to that which is desultory, which is insignificant in itself. And therefore, when the scratches in my manuscript cried, like sinners, for salvation, and assailed my eyes with the ugliness of their irrelevance, I often took more time in rescuing them into a merciless finality of rhythm than in carrying on what was my obvious task."[5]

This understanding of rhythm is the reason behind success in art, which Rabindranath started enjoying later on. He expressed this feeling in a letter to Rothenstein in 1937 "I have been havoc in the complacent and stagnant world of Indian art and my people are puzzled for they do not know what judgement to pronounce upon my picture. But, I must say enjoying hugely my role as a painter."[6] This was also recognized by European reviewers like Henri Bidou, as they were impressed with Tagore's naïve 'automatic' self-taught quality, especially as they were aware of his high quality formal 'mimetic' literary output. Art critique Coomaraswamy was convinced that Rabindranath had expunged all previous literary experience to produce a truly naïve art, like a child, inventing his own technique.[7] Besides the vision of rhythm and child like quality Rabindranath had two other elements, unpredictability and dream imagination. This is expressed by Rabindranath in 1930 *"People often ask me about the meaning of my pictures. I remain silent even as they are. It is for them to express not to explain…."*[8]

Methodology and Data Analysis

A biblometric study of 1573 drawings and paintings of Rabindranath in the custody of Rabindra Bhavana at Santiniketan is made on different aspects such as theme, medium used, signature, place and date of drawing, titles given by him. This would help to have an idea about Tagore as a painter.

Table 8.1: Theme of the Paintings in Tagoreana

Sl. No.	*Themes*	*No. of Paintings*	*Percentage*
1.	Figures	496	31.532
2	Human face	219	13.922
3.	Head study	206	13.096
4.	Landscape	173	10.998
5.	Animal	63	4.005
6.	Bird	62	3.941
7.	Design	58	3.687
8.	Composition	54	3.433
9.	Illustration for books etc. (30 for the book *Khapchhada*)	49	3.115
10.	Mask	40	2.543
11.	Different forms	40	2.543
12.	Sketch	29	1.844
13.	Flower study	26	1.653
14.	Nude study (Female 11, Male 4)	15	0.954
15.	Portrait	14	0.890
16.	Flower	8	0.509
17.	Couple	8	0.509
18.	Fish	4	0.254
19.	Fish and a cat	1	0.063
20.	Plant study	1	0.063
21.	Two pine trees	1	0.063
22.	Tree	1	0.063
23.	Croton leaf	1	0.063
24.	Steam engine	1	0.063
25.	Animal head	1	0.063
26.	Hut	1	0.063
27.	Wild face	1	0.063
	Total	**1573**	**100.00**

Source: Tagore's Drawings and Paintings of Rabindra Bhavana.

The broad categorization of Tagore's paintings made on the basis of descriptive catalogue of Rabindra Bhavana and experts' opinion reveal that Rabindranath drew on 27 themes. A detail analytical study of the themes is made here under:

Table 8.2: Paintings of Figures in Tagoreana

Sl. No.	*Themes*	*No. of Painting*	*Percentage*
1	Human figure	249	50.201
2.	Standing figure	71	14.315
3.	Figure-seated	34	6.855
4.	Bearded man	22	4.435

(*Contd.*)

Sl. No.	Themes	No. of Painting	Percentage
5.	Dancing figure	15	3.024
6.	Man with a raised hand	12	2.419
7.	An old man with a stick	6	1.210
8.	Man with a cap	4	0.806
9.	Figure on a coach	4	0.806
10.	Figure with animal head	3	0.605
11.	Couple	3	0.605
12.	Man with a torch	3	0.605
13.	Man -knelling	3	0.605
14.	Old man with a mirror	3	0.605
15.	Woman under a tree	3	0.605
16.	Woman and a child	2	0.403
17.	Man with a girl	2	0.403
18.	Woman with a veena	2	0.403
19.	An old man riding on a bird	2	0.403
20.	Mother and a child	2	0.403
21.	Lady with a mirror in hand	1	0.201
22.	Lady with a lamp	1	0.201
23.	Lady with a flower	1	0.201
24.	Female figure with a pot on shoulder	1	0.201
25.	A walking man	1	0.201
26.	Man with a musical instrument	1	0.201
27.	Woman absorbed in painting	1	0.201
28.	Woman seating with a picture in hand	1	0.201
29.	Man in a long robe	1	0.201
30.	Running figure	1	0.201
31.	Lovers	1	0.201
32.	Woman in woods	1	0.201
33.	An old man blending	1	0.201
34.	Lady with a pot	1	0.201
35.	Woman and rain	1	0.201
36.	A man standing with a sword	1	0.201
37.	An old man standing	1	0.201
38.	Men in armor	1	0.201
39.	A couple with a camel	1	0.201
40.	Woman on a animal	1	0.201
41.	Woman on a cot	1	0.201
42.	Man playing a drum	1	0.201
43.	Man with spectacles	1	0.201
44.	A man seated by waterside	1	0.201
45.	A man with a goat	1	0.201
46.	Woman standing at window	1	0.201
47.	Two men fighting	1	0.201
48.	Man with a cock	1	0.201
49.	One man blessing other	1	0.201
50.	Man with a pole	1	0.201
51.	Study of a boy in profile	1	0.201
52.	Man with a helmet	1	0.201
53.	Woman heavily ornamented	1	0.201

(Contd.)

Sl. No.	*Themes*	*No. of Painting*	*Percentage*
54.	Woman in black dress	1	0.201
55.	Woman behind a hillock	1	0.201
56.	Woman on a sofa	1	0.201
57.	Woman with closed eyes	1	0.201
58.	An old man and a child	1	0.201
59.	Female figure with a bird	1	0.201
60.	Wild figure	1	0.201
61.	Two figure and a poem	1	0.201
62.	Man and woman	1	0.201
63.	Man in the back of a bird in flight	1	0.201
64.	Boy with a stick	1	0.201
65.	Woman-bathing	1	0.201
66.	Woman in a boat	1	0.201
67.	Boat and a man	1	0.201
68.	Bull and a man	1	0.201
69.	Woman carrying a picture	1	0.201
70.	Man with a dog	1	0.201
71.	Woman nursing a sick person	1	0.201
	Total	**496**	**100.00**

Source: Tagore's Drawings and Paintings of Rabindra Bhavana.

Table 8.3: Paintings of Human Faces in Tagoreana

Sl. No.	*Themes*	*No. of Paintings*	*Percentage*
1.	Human face (male & female)	200	91.324
2.	Bearded face	10	4.566
3.	Face study	3	1.370
4.	Human face-design	2	0.913
5.	Face of a man with a cap	2	0.913
6.	Human face and a fish	1	0.457
7.	Mask like face	1	0.457
	Total	**219**	**100.00**

Source: Tagore's Drawings and Paintings of Rabindra Bhavana.

Table 8.4: Paintings of Animals in Tagoreana

Sl. No.	*Themes*	*No. of Paintings*	*Percentage*
1.	Animal fantasy	17	26.984
2.	Animal(s)	14	22.222
3.	Dog	10	15.873
4.	Cow	3	4.762
5.	Animal head	3	4.762
6.	Fox	2	3.175
7.	Elephant	2	3.175

(Contd.)

Sl. No.	Themes	No. of Paintings	Percentage
8.	Jackal—illustration for "Se"	2	3.175
9.	Deer	1	1.587
10.	Crocodile	1	1.587
11.	Camel like	1	1.587
12.	Two serpents	1	1.587
13.	Two alligators	1	1.587
14.	Two animals- one rodent and one bird	1	1.587
15.	Animal in a forest	1	1.587
16.	Animal inside a bowl	1	1.587
17.	Animal face	1	1.587
18.	Rabbit	1	1.587
	Total	**63**	**100.00**

Source: Tagore's Drawings and Paintings of Rabindra Bhavana.

Table 8.5: Paintings of Birds in Tagoreana

Sl. No.	Themes	No. of Paintings	Percentage
1.	Birds (from and shape)	36	58.065
2.	Bird-design	8	12.903
3.	Bird in flight	3	4.839
4.	Birds and animals	3	4.839
5.	Bird-fantasy	2	3.226
6.	Owl	2	3.226
7.	Birds on the sea weaves	1	1.613
8.	Birds on a geometric form	1	1.613
9.	Bird and a bearded man	1	1.613
10.	Birds and reptiles	1	1.613
11.	Two peacocks	1	1.613
12.	Duck	1	1.613
13.	Cock	1	1.613
14.	Crane	1	1.613
	Total	**62**	**100.00**

Source: Tagore's Drawings and Paintings of Rabindra Bhavana.

Table 8.6: Drawing of Designs in Tagoreana

Sl. No.	Themes	No. of Paintings	Percentage
1.	Bearded man	16	27.586
2.	Design	15	25.862
3.	Design of a sitting figure	5	8.620
4.	Water pot	3	5.172
5.	Architectural design with a face	3	5.172
6.	Design of a man	3	5.172
7.	Animal	2	3.448

(Contd.)

Sl. No.	Themes	No. of Paintings	Percentage
8.	Human figure inside a design	2	3.448
9.	Design resembling a face	2	3.448
10.	Human head	1	1.724
11.	Tray	1	1.724
12.	Dancing figure with a design	1	1.724
13.	Fish-design	1	1.724
14.	Design over a poem	1	1.724
15.	Design of a oval shaped horse	1	1.724
16.	Design with Bengali script	1	1.724
	Total	**58**	**100.00**

Source: Tagore's Drawings and Paintings of Rabindra Bhavana.

Table 8.7: Paintings of Compositions in Tagoreana

Sl. No.	Themes	No. of Paintings	Percentage
1.	Figure composition (two-seven fig)	43	79.630
2.	Man and a boy	1	1.852
3.	Two figures with a child	1	1.852
4.	Worship of a primitive idol	1	1.852
5.	Male figure riding on a crocodile	1	1.852
6.	Donkey in a forest	1	1.852
7.	Composition- Chandraloke	1	1.852
8.	Composition with a woman face	1	1.852
9.	Colour composition	1	1.852
10.	Man and a boat	1	1.852
11.	Composition with birds	1	1.852
12.	Composition with architecture	1	1.852
	Total	**54**	**100.00**

Source: Tagore's Drawings and Paintings of Rabindra Bhavana.

Table 8.8: Illustrations for Khapchhada

Sl. No.	Themes	No. of Paintings	Percentage
1.	Face of woman/man	5	16.667
2.	Figure-standing	2	6.667
3.	Head	2	6.667
4.	Matilal Nandi	1	3.333
5.	Narahari Sharma	1	3.333
6.	Kabi-adhunik	1	3.333
7.	Two figures	1	3.333
8.	Leg being brushed	1	3.333
9.	Rannar Sab Thik	1	3.333
10.	Badsa	1	3.333
11.	M.Sc.	1	3.333

(*Contd.*)

Sl. No.	Themes	No. of Paintings	Percentage
12.	Chhato Bau	1	3.333
13.	Sindhkata	1	3.333
14.	Potter Khudu	1	3.333
15.	Baneswar	1	3.333
15.	Mukh dheke	1	3.333
16.	Neyamat Darji	1	3.333
17.	Daktar	1	3.333
18.	Man with a raised hand	1	3.333
19.	Smiling face	1	3.333
20.	Demodar Seth	1	3.333
21.	Girl with a ear ring	1	3.333
22.	Penehu	1	3.333
23.	Adhkhana-Bel	1	3.333
	Total	**30**	**100.00**

Source: Tagore's Drawings and Paintings of Rabindra Bhavana.

Table 8.9: Different Form of Paintings in Tagoreana

Sl. No.	Themes	No. of Paintings	Percentage
1.	Zoomorphic form	15	37.500
2.	Animal form	9	22.500
3.	Geometric form	6	15.000
4.	Reptile	3	7.500
5.	Angular forın	3	7.500
6.	Snake like form - fantasy	1	2.500
7.	Silhovette form	1	2.500
8.	Composite form	1	2.500
9.	Two forms	1	2.500
	Total	**40**	**100.00**

Source: Tagore's Drawings and Paintings of Rabindra Bhavana.

Table 8.10: Different Types of Sketch in Tagoreana

Sl. No.	Themes	No. of Paintings	Percentage
1.	Coloured sketch	12	41.379
2.	Woman sketch	4	13.793
3.	A woman at the door	2	6.897
4.	Two human figures	2	6.897
5.	Sketch	1	3.448
6.	An old man	1	3.448
7.	A man with a cap	1	3.448
8.	Man with a turban	1	3.448
9.	Five faces	1	3.448
10.	Taimurlong sketch of a boy	1	3.448

(Contd.)

Sl. No.	Themes	No. of Paintings	Percentage
11.	Woman in a net	1	3.448
12.	Khudiram sketch of a boy	1	3.448
13.	Sketch incomplete	1	3.448
	Total	**29**	**100.00**

Source: Tagore's Drawings and Paintings of Rabindra Bhavana.

Table 8.11: Portrait in Tagoreana

Sl. No.	Themes	No. of Paintings	Percentage
1.	Portrait of a woman	7	50.000
2.	Self portrait	4	28.571
3.	Portrait of a man	2	14.286
4.	Turbaned head	1	7.143
	Total	**14**	**100.00**

Source: Tagore's Drawings and Paintings of Rabindra Bhavana.

From above Tables (8.1 to 8.11) an idea about 27 different themes of Rabindranath's paintings can be studied. And by analysing the themes it can be noticed that at least on 177 different sub-themes Rabindranath drawn paintings which cover different animals, birds, design, sketch, composition, forms and illustrations.

Rabindranath used various medium for drawing his paintings. He used pen ink, waterproof ink, crayon, water colour, pastel colour and pencil in different combination. The varieties of combination are as follows:

Table 8.12: Use of Pen ink, Pen ink with other Mediums in Paintings

Sl. No.	Colour combination	No. of Paintings	Percentage
1.	Pen ink	466	71.145
2.	Pen ink with read pen and brush	44	6.713
3.	Pen ink and water colour	31	4.733
4.	Pen ink and poster colour	29	4.427
5.	Pen ink and crayon	21	3.206
6.	Pen ink, water colour and waterproof ink	11	1.679
7.	Pen ink and brush work	11	1.679
8.	Pen ink with pencil underlining	9	1.374

(*Contd.*)

Sl. No.	Colour combination	No. of Paintings	Percentage
9.	Pen ink with read pen	7	1.069
10.	Pen ink and pastel colour	6	0.916
11.	Pen ink, crayon and pastel	5	0.763
12.	Pen ink, water colour and poster colour	4	0.611
13.	Pen ink, poster colour and pastel	2	0.305
14.	Pen ink, poster colour and crayon	2	0.305
15.	Pen ink and gold ink	1	0.153
16.	Pen ink , poster white with brush	1	0.153
17.	Pen ink, water colour, poster colour and pastel	1	0.153
18.	Pen ink, poster colour and water colour	1	0.153
19.	Pen ink, waterproof ink with bush	1	0.153
20.	Pen ink, water colour and golden colour	1	0.153
21.	Pen ink and vegetable colour	1	0.153
	Total	**655**	**100.00**

Source: Tagore's Drawings and Paintings of Rabindra Bhavana.

Table 8.13: Use of Waterproof ink, Waterproof ink with other Mediums in Paintings

Sl. No.	Colour combination	No. of Paintings	Percentage
1.	Waterproof ink	218	30.748
2.	Waterproof ink and pen ink	216	30.465
3.	Waterproof ink and poster colour	102	14.386
4.	Waterproof ink, pen ink and poster colour	63	8.886
5.	Waterproof ink, pen ink, brush and pen work	24	3.385
6.	Waterproof ink and water colour	20	2.820
7.	Waterproof ink and crayon	9	1.269
8.	Waterproof ink and pastel	8	1.128
9.	Waterproof ink, poster colour and pastel	4	0.564
10.	Waterproof ink, poster colour and crayon	4	0.564
11.	Waterproof ink, poster colour and water colour	4	0.564
12.	Waterproof ink and gauche	4	0.564
13.	Waterproof ink, brush and read handling	3	0.423
14.	Waterproof ink and brush work	3	0.423
15.	Waterproof ink, pen ink and crayon	3	0.423
16.	Waterproof ink and pen ink with read pen	3	0.423
17.	Waterproof ink with link and wash handling	2	0.282
18.	Waterproof ink, pen ink, poster and pastel	2	0.282
19.	Waterproof ink, pen ink and pastel	2	0.282
20.	Waterproof ink, pen ink with gold dust with glue	2	0.282
21.	Waterproof ink and pencil	2	0.282
22.	Waterproof ink, poster colour, crayon and pen ink	2	0.282
23.	Waterproof ink with varnish	2	0.282

(Contd.)

Sl. No.	Colour combination	No. of Paintings	Percentage
24.	Waterproof ink with pen and brush	1	0.141
25.	Waterproof ink, poster colour, pen ink with brush and pen	1	0.141
26.	Waterproof ink, pen ink, water colour and pastel	1	0.141
27.	Waterproof ink, water colour and pastel	1	0.141
28.	Waterproof ink, water colour, pen ink and poster colour	1	0.141
29.	Waterproof ink over charcoal drawing	1	0.141
30.	Waterproof ink, water colour with crayon	1	0.141
	Total	**709**	**100.00**

Source: Tagore's Drawings and Paintings of Rabindra Bhavana.

Table 8.14: Use of Crayon, Crayon with other Mediums in Paintings

Sl. No.	Colour combination	No. of Paintings	Percentage
1.	Crayon	52	64.198
2.	Crayon and pastel colour	24	29.630
3.	Crayon and pencil	3	3.704
4.	Crayon and water colour	1	1.235
5.	Crayon, pastel and waterproof ink	1	1.235
	Total	**81**	**100.00**

Source: Tagore's Drawings and Paintings of Rabindra Bhavana.

Table 8.15: Use of Water Colour, Water Colour with Other Mediums in Paintings

Sl. No.	Colour combination	No. of Paintings	Percentage
1.	Water colour	16	37.209
2.	Water colour and pen ink	11	25.581
3.	Water colour and poster colour	4	9.302
4.	Water colour and waterproof ink	4	9.302
5.	Water colour, ink and brush work	3	6.977
6.	Water colour and pastel	2	4.651
7.	Water colour and brush handling	1	2.326
8.	Water colour, waterproof ink and crayon	1	2.326
9.	Water colour, pen ink with crayon	1	2.326
	Total	**43**	**100.00**

Source: Tagore's Drawings and Paintings of Rabindra Bhavana.

Table 8.16: Use of Pastel, Pastel with other Mediums in Paintings

Sl. No.	*Colour combination*	*No. of Paintings*	*Percentage*
1.	Pastel and pen ink	11	40.741
2.	Pastel	8	29.630
3.	Pastel, waterproof ink and poster colour	2	7.407
4.	Pastel and pencil	2	7.407
5.	Pastel, pen ink and pencil	1	3.703
6.	Pastel, pen wash with water colour	1	3.703
7.	Pastel and poster colour	1	3.703
8.	Pastel, crayon, pen and water colour	1	3.703
	Total	**27**	**100.00**

Source: Tagore's Drawings and Paintings of Rabindra Bhavana.

8.17: Use of Pencil, Pencil with other Mediums in Paintings

Sl. No.	*Colour combination*	*No. of Paintings*	*Percentage*
1.	Pencil	31	88.571
2.	Pencil with pastel and crayon	2	5.714
3.	Pencil, poster colour and waterproof ink	1	2.857
4.	Pencil, crayon and pen ink	1	2.857
	Total	**35**	**100.00**

Source: Tagore's Drawings and Paintings of Rabindra Bhavana.

Table 8.18: Use of Other Mediums in Paintings

Sl. No.	*Colour combination*	*No. of Paintings*	*Percentage*
1.	Poster colour	13	56.522
2.	Etching print	5	21.739
3.	Etching print Gouache (5 on paper and 1 on silk)	4	17.391
4.	Vegetable colour	1	4.348
	Total	**23**	**100.00**

Source: Tagore's Drawings and Paintings of Rabindra Bhavana.

From Tables (8.12 to 8.18) varieties of medium used by Rabindranath in drawing his paintings can be traced. Actually Rabindranath used to combine different medium in his drawings and paintings instead of using single medium. For example Tagore used exclusively pen ink in 466 (71.145%) paintings out of 655 paintings where pen ink was used. It can be noticed that

Rabindranath used pen ink with 21 combinations, waterproof ink with 30 combinations, crayon with 5 combinations, water colour with 9 combinations and pastel and pencil with 8 and 4 combinations respectively.

Rabindranath used various canvases for paintings and drawings which can be traced out from the following Tables (8.19 to 8.32).

Table 8.19: Canvas used in Paintings of Tagoreana

Sl. No.	*Painted on*	*No. of Paintings*	*Percentage*
1.	Plain paper	1524	96.884
2.	Other than plain paper	49	3.115
	Total	**1573**	**100.00**

Source: Tagore's Drawings and Paintings of Rabindra Bhavana.

Table 8.20: Works on Different Canvas other than Paper in Paintings of Tagoreana

Sl. No.	*Painted on*	*No. of Paintings*	*Percentage*
1	Printed on Visva-Bharati News[9]	12	24.490
2.	Card	9	18.367
3.	Silk	6	12.245
4.	Wood	5	10.204
5.	Wooden box	5	10.204
6.	Wooden board	4	8.163
7.	Varnished paper	2	4.082
8.	Pasted card	2	4.082
9.	Glazed paper	1	2.041
10.	Exercise book	1	2.041
11.	Backside of a letter	1	2.041
12.	Pasted paper	1	2.041
	Total	**49**	**100.00**

Source: Tagore's Drawings and Paintings of Rabindra Bhavana.

Table 8.21: Paintings on Visva-Bharati News

Sl. No.	*Medium*	*No. of Paintings*	*Percentage*
1.	Pen ink and water colour	5	41.667
2.	Pen ink and poster colour	2	16.667
3.	Pen ink and pastel	2	16.667
4.	Pen ink	1	8.333

(Contd.)

Sl. No.	Medium	No. of Paintings	Percentage
5.	Pastel and water colour	1	8.333
6.	Pastel, crayon, pencil, pen and water colour	1	8.333
	Total (12 sketch)	**12**	**100.00**

Source: Tagore's Drawings and Paintings of Rabindra Bhavana.

Table 8.22: Paintings on Card

Sl. No.	Themes	Medium	No. of paintings	Percentage
1.	Head study	1 Pen ink, 1 lead pencil	2	22.222
2.	Face	2 Pen ink	2	22.222
3.	Bearded man	1 Pen ink	1	11.111
4.	Male figure	1 Pen ink	1	11.111
5.	Female figure	1 Pen ink	1	11.111
6.	Woman on a sofa	1 Pen ink	1	11.111
7.	Chitralipi	1 Water colour	1	11.111
	Total		**9**	**100.00**

Source: Tagore's Drawings and Paintings of Rabindra Bhavana.

Table 8.23: Paintings on Silk

Sl. No.	Themes	Medium	No. of Paintings	Percentage
1.	Head study— woman	1 Gouche colour, 1 water pcof ink, 1 water colour	3	50.000
2.	Animal	1 Water proof ink	1	16.667
3.	Landscape	1 Pastel and pen ink	1	16.667
4.	Dancing girl	1 Crayon and pen	1	16.667
	Total		**6**	**100.00**

Source: Tagore's Drawings and Paintings of Rabindra Bhavana.

Table 8.24: Paintings on Wood

Sl. No.	Themes	Medium	No. of Paintings	Percentage
1.	Seated woman	2 Pen ink and waterproof ink	2	40.000
2.	Owl	1 Pen ink and water colour	1	20.000
3.	Man playing down	1 Pen ink and water colour	1	20.000
4.	Mask like figure	1 Poster colour, waterproof ink, pen ink	1	20.000
	Total		**5**	**100.00**

Source: Tagore's Drawings and Paintings of Rabindra Bhavana.

Table 8.25: Paintings on Wooden Box

Sl. No.	*Themes*	*Medium*	*No. of Paintings*	*Percentage*
1.	Bird	2 Pen ink and waterproof ink	2	40.000
2.	Face of a bearded man	1 Pen ink and waterproof ink	1	20.000
3.	Face in profile	1 Pen ink, waterproof and water colour ink	1	20.000
4.	Composition with architecture	1 Water colour and waterproof ink	1	20.000
	Total		**5**	**100.00**

Source: Tagore's Drawings and Paintings of Rabindra Bhavana.

Table 8.26: Paintings on Wooden Board

Sl. No	*Themes*	*Medium*	*No. of Paintings*	*Percentage*
1.	Landscape	1 Pen ink, waterproof ink and poster colour	1	25.000
2.	Bearded man	1 Waterproof ink, pen ink and poster colour	1	25.000
3.	Standing figure	1 waterproof ink, pen ink and poster colour	1	25.000
4.	Tree	1 Water colour, waterproof ink and pen ink	1	25.000
	Total		**4**	**100.00**

Source: Tagore's Drawings and Paintings of Rabindra Bhavana.

Table 8.27: Paintings on Varnished Paper

Sl. No.	*Theme*	*Medium*	*No. of Paintings*	*Percentage*
1.	Face of a woman	1 Water colour and waterproof ink	1	50.000
2.	Head study-profile	1 Water colour and waterproof ink	1	50.000
	Total		**2**	**100.00**

Source: Tagore's Drawings and Paintings of Rabindra Bhavana.

Table 8.28: Paintings on Pasted Card

Sl. No.	Themes	Medium	No. of Paintings	Percentage
1.	Face of a woman	1 Pen ink	1	50.000
2.	Mask like face	1 Pen ink	1	50.000
	Total		**2**	**100.00**

Source: Tagore's Drawings and Paintings of Rabindra Bhavana.

Table 8.29: Paintings on Glazed Paper

Sl. No.	Theme	Medium	No. of Painting	Percentage
1.	Narabudbud	1 waterproof ink	1	100.00

Source: Tagore's Drawings and Paintings of Rabindra Bhavana.

Table 8.30: Painting in Exercise Book

Sl. No.	Theme	Medium	No. of Paintings	Percentage
1.	Design over a poem	1 Pen ink	1	100.00

Source: Tagore's Drawings and Paintings of Rabindra Bhavana.

Table 8.31: Painting on backside of a Paper

Sl. No.	Theme	Medium	No. of Painting	Percentage
1.	Flower	1 Pen ink	1	100.00

Source: Tagore's Drawings and Paintings of Rabindra Bhavana.

Table 8.32: Painting on Pasted Paper

Sl. No.	Theme	Medium	No. of Painting	Percentage
1.	Flower study	1 Pen ink and water colour	1	100.00

Source: Tagore's Drawings and Paintings of Rabindra Bhavana.

It can be observed that Rabindranath mostly used paper as a medium in 1524 paintings out of 1573 paintings, but for remaining 49 paintings under study he used 12 other different mediums including Visva-Bharati News. The theme of paintings drawn on canvas other than paper includes human figure, bird, composition, tree, flower, landscape etc.

To authenticate his drawings and paintings Rabindranath used to put his different types of signature in different language on it. An account of signature used by Rabindranath on his paintings and drawings is given in Tables 8.33 to 8.37.

Table 8.33: Signature of Rabindranath Tagore on Paintings

Sl. No.	*Signature*	*No. of Paintings*	*Percentage*
1.	Signed	958	60.903
2..	Unsigned	615	39.097
	Total	**1573**	**100.00**

Source: Tagore's Drawings and Paintings of Rabindra Bhavana.

Table 8.34: Signature of Rabindranath Tagore in different Language on Paintings

Sl. No.	*Signature*	*No. of Paintings*	*Percentage*
1.	Bengali	903	94.259
2.	English	53	5.532
3.	Bengali and English both	2	0.209
	Total	**958**	**100.00**

Source: Tagore's Drawings and Paintings of Rabindra Bhavana.

Table 8.35: Types of Bengali Signature of Rabindranath Tagore on Paintings

Sl. No.	*Signature*	*No. of Paintings*	*Percentage*
1.	"Rabindra"	571	63.234
2.	"Sri Rabindra"	299	33.112
3.	" Rabindranath"	13	1.440
4.	" Sri Rabindranath Thakur"	9	0.997
5.	"Rabindranath Thakur"	5	0.554
6.	" Rabindra" and also " Ra Tha"	1	0.111
7.	"Sri Rabindra" and "Rabindra"	1	0.111
8.	"Ra Tha"	1	0.111
9.	"Rabi Dada"	1	0.111
10.	"Ra Tha" and "Sri Rabindranath Tagore"	1	0.111
11.	"Sri Rabindra" and "Rabindranath Tagore"	1	0.111
	Total	**903**	**100.00**

Source: Tagore's Drawings and Paintings of Rabindra Bhavana.

Table 8.36: Types of English Signature of Rabindranath Tagore on Paintings

Sl. No.	*Signature*	*No. of Paintings*	*Percentage*
1.	"Rabindranath"	24	45.283
2.	"Rabindra"	18	33.962
3.	"Rabindranath Tagore"	9	16.981
4.	"Sri Rabindra"	2	3.774
	Total	**53**	**100.00**

Source: Tagore's Drawings and Paintings of Rabindra Bhavana.

Table 8.37: Combination of English and Bengali Signature of Rabindranath Tagore on Paintings

Sl. No.	*Signature*	*No. of Paintings*	*Percentage*
1.	"Sri Rabindranath Tagore" in Bengali script and "Rabindranath Tagore" in Roman Script	1	50.000
2..	"Rabindra" in Bengali Script and "Rabindranath" in Roman Script	1	50.000
	Total	**2**	**100.00**

Source: Tagore's Drawings and Paintings of Rabindra Bhavana.

It may be observed from Tables 8.33 to 8.37 that Rabindranath put his signature in 958 occasions predominantly as Rabindra (63.234%) and in Bengali (94.259%).

Rabindranath extensively travelled throughout the world besides India. Rabindranath used to write name of the place and date in his writings. But in case of paintings place of paintings mentioned in the paintings is less as noticed from the following Tables 8.38 to 8.43:

Table 8.38: Place of Painting

Sl. No.	*Place*	*No. of Paintings*	*Percentage*
1.	Not mentioned	1525	96.949
2.	Mentioned	48	3.051
	Total	**1573**	**100.00**

Source: Tagore's Drawings and Paintings of Rabindra Bhavana.

Table 8.39: Place of Paintings Mentioned in Tagoreana

Sl. No.	*Place*	*No. of Paintings*	*Percentage*
1.	Indian	29	60.417
2.	Foreign	19	39.583
	Total	**48**	**100.00**

Source: Tagore's Drawings and Paintings of Rabindra Bhavana.

Table 8.40: Indian Places of Paintings Mentioned in Tagoreana

Sl. No.	*Place*	*No. of Paintings*	*Percentage*
1.	Adihar	11	37.932
2.	Santiniketan	7	24.138
3.	Hyderabad	5	17.242
4.	Mongpu	1	3.448
5.	Darjeeling	1	3.448
6.	Chandannagar	1	3.448
7.	Jarasanko	1	3.448
8.	Kalingpong	1	3.448
9.	Delhi	1	3.448
	Total	**29**	**100.00**

Source: Tagore's Drawings and Paintings of Rabindra Bhavana.

Table 8.41: Foreign Places of Paintings Mentioned in Tagoreana

Sl. No.	*Place*	*No. of Paintings*	*Percentage*
1.	Moscow	7	36.842
2.	Lahore	5	26.316
3.	S S Taiyomary (Sanfrancesco)	3	15.790
4.	Baghdad	1	5.263
5.	Sanghai	1	5.263
6.	Tehran	1	5.263
7.	S S Angers	1	5.263
	Total	**19**	**100.00**

Table 8.42: Dates of Paintings where Place Mentioned: India

Sl. No.	*Place*	*Dates of Paintings*	*No. of Paintings*
1.	Adihar	19.10.1934, 22.10.1934, 23.10.1934, 25.10.1934, 26.20.1934, 29.10.1934, 30.10.1934, November 1934	11
2.	Santiniketan	22.5.1931, 17.11.1933, 20.8.1934, November 1934, 20.12.1934, 6.4.1935, 6.9.1935	7

(Contd.)

Sl. No.	Place	Dates of Paintings	No. of Paintings
3.	Hyderabad	12.12.1933, 18.12.1933 (2), 23.12.1933, 24.12.1933	5
4.	Mangpu	17.6.1939	1
5.	Darjeeling	November 1931	1
6.	Chandannagar	3.11.1933	1
7.	Jarasanko	30.12.1933	1
8.	Delhi	3.11.1936	1
9.	Kalingpong	September 1940	1
	Total		**29**

Note: Number within bracket indicated number of paintings in a day.
Source: Tagore's Drawings and Paintings of Rabindra Bhavana.

Table 8.43: Dates of Paintings where Place Mentioned: Foreign

Sl. No.	Place	Dates of Paintings	No. of Paintings
1.	Moscow	15.9.1930(4), 16.9.1930, 19.9.1930, September 1930	7
2.	Lahore	24.2.1935(2), 25.2.1935(2), 27.1.1935	5
3.	S S Taiyomaru	21.4.1929,26.4.1929, one no date	3
4.	Baghdad	12.5.1932	1
5.	Sanghai	17.3.1929	1
6.	Tehran	6.5.1932	1
7.	SS Angers	6.10.1929	1
	Total		**19**

Note: Number within bracket indicated number of paintings in a day.
Source: Tagore's Drawings and Paintings of Rabindra Bhavana.

A quick look into Tables (4.38 to 8.43) reveals that Rabindranath mentioned place of paintings only in case of 48 occasions (i.e. in 3.051% of his paintings) which are predominantly India (29 places, i.e. 60.417%). But all the paintings with dates, place of drawing also mentioned.

Dates on any writing help to draw a chronological development of writings or ideas. But paintings in Tagoreana lacks date in 1100 occasions (i.e. 69.930% of Tagore's paintings) as identified from Tables 8.44 to 8.46.

Table 8.44: Date of Paintings

Sl. No.	Date	No. of Paintings	Percentage
1.	Date not mentioned	1100	69.930
2.	Date mentioned	473	30.070
	Total	**1573**	**100.00**

Table 8.45: Year-wise Production of Dated Paintings

Sl. No.	Year	No. of Paintings	Percentage
1.	1929	6	1.418
2.	1930	8	1.891
3.	1931	11	2.600
4.	1932	25	5.910
5.	1933	20	4.728
6.	1934	57	13.475
7.	1935	61	14.421
8.	1936	65	15.366
9.	1937	53	12.520
10.	1938	48	11.348
11.	1939	60	14.184
12.	1940	9	2.177
	Total	**423**	**100.00**

Table 8.46: Date-wise Production of Dated Paintings

Sl. No.	Year	Date of Paintings	No.
1.	1929	15.3, 21.3, 21.4, 25.4, 26.4, 1929	6
2.	1930	15.9 (3), 16.9, 18.9, 19.9, Sept (2)	8
3.	1931	13.1 (2), 10.3, March, 2.5, 19.5, May (2), June, November,1931	11
4.	1932	January, 1.2, 2.3 (3), 5.3, 6.3, March (6), April, 6.5, 12.5, May, 1932 (8)	25
5.	1933	March, 15.9, 1.11, 2.11, 3.11 (2), 17.11, 18.11 (2), 31.11, 7.12, 8.12, 12.12, 15.12, 18.2 (2), 2.12, 24.12, 31.12 (2)	20
6.	1934	6.1 (3), 12.1 (3), 13.1 (2), 6.1 (4), 21.1 (2), 22.1, 24.1, 27.1, 30.1, 7.4, 9.4, May, 20.6, 3.7, 19.7, 7.10, 10.10, 15.10, 16.10 (3), 19.10, 22.10, 23.10, 24.10 (2), 25.10 (5), 26.10, 27.10, 28.10, 29.10 (2), 30.10 (2), 31.10, 10.11, 12.11, 27.11, Nov (3), 20.2, December (2)	57
7.	1935	31.1 (2), 1.2, 17.2, 18.2, 22.2, 24.2, 25.2 (2), 27.2 (3),17.3, 6.4, 10.4 (2), 14.4 (2), 18.4, April, 4.5, 5.5 (2), 5.6, 13.6, 23.6 (2), 9.7 (2), 20.7, 24.7 (2), 28.7, 9.8, 19.8 (2), 22.8 (2), 25.8, 28.8, August, 6.9, 21.9, 14.10 (3), 15.10, 30.10, 31.10, 2.11, 4.11, 7.11 (5), 8.11, 10.11, 14.11, 6.12, 1935.	61

(Contd.)

Sl. No.	Year	Date of Paintings	No.
8.	1936	January, 1.3, 3.3, 3.4, 5.4 (2), 16.4, 24.4 (2), 11.5, 14.5 (2), 15.5 (3), 16.5 (2), 18.5, 19.5 (2), 20.5 (2), 21.5 (3), 20.6 (4), 26.6 (2), 28.6 (6), 30.6, June, 20.7, 1.8, 3.8 (3), 16.8 (2), 23.8, 10.10, 17.10, 20.10 (2), 3.11, 5.11 (2), 6.11, 7.11 (3), 11.11, 1936 (6)	65
9.	1937	1.3, 20.3, 29.3, 5.4, 6.4, 8.4, 9.4 (2), 10.4, 15.4, 23.6, 27.6, 13.9, 21.9 (2), 22.9 (3), 25.9 (2), 26.9, 27.9 (2), 3.10 (2), 5.10, 9.10 (3), 10.10 (2), 19.10, 20.10, 23.10, 6.11 (3), 7.11 (2), 8.11 (2), 9.11 (3), 10.11, 15.11, 6.12 (3), 16.12, 1937 (3)	53
10.	1938	22.1, 9.2 (2), 25.2 (4), March (3), 3.4, 5.4 (2), 7.4 (2), 17.4, 24.4, 27.4, 25.6, 1.10, 15.10, 2.11 (2), 7.11 (4), November, 20.12, 1938 (19)	48
11.	1939	15.1, 22.1, 29.1, 19.2 (2), 20.2 (2), 21.2, 22.2 (4), 26.2 (2), 2.3, 21.3 (2), 5.6, 13.6, 15.6, 16.6 (2), 17.6, 20.6, 22.6, 23.6, 20.7 (4), 26.7, 8.11, 9.11, 11.11, 13.11, 16.11, November (2), 3.12, 1939 (21)	60
12.	1940	5.4, 12.4, 16.4, 5.5, 210.5, 13.6, September, 5.9, 3.11.	9

Note: Number within bracket indicates number of paintings in a date/month etc.

Source: Tagore's Drawings and Paintings of Rabindra Bhavana.

It may be recorded from the available dates that first paintings drawn on 15th March, 1929 and last one on 3rd November, 1939. But as Rabindranath put date only in 473 in numbers (i.e. 30% of total paintings) it would not be possible to identify chronology of paintings in Tagoreana.

Rabindranath gave title to his drawings and paintings only in 46 occasions as indicated in Table 8.47.

Table 8.47: Titles of Paintings Given by Rabindranath

Sl. No.	Titles	Theme	Size in cm.	Date
1.	"Suo Rani Duo Rani"	Flower study	21.5 × 33	
2.	"Jantur juju"		42 × 9.5	17.11.1937
3.	"Chandraloke"	Composition	25 × 31.5	March 1931
4.	"Chandar Khata"	Zoomorphic form	14.6 × 23	
5.	"Galpa-Salpa"	Group of figures	21 × 29	September 1940
6.	"Chitralipi"		13.2 × 20.5	
7.	"Baibahik"	Standing figure	17 × 20	
8.	"Consoler"		20.5 × 35.5	
9.	"Pollaram"	Man with a stick	21.5 × 36.4	

(Contd.)

Sl. No.	Titles	Theme	Size in cm.	Date
10.	"Nara bud bud"		18.5 × 23	
11.	"Hasi"	Head of an animal	11 × 19	
12.	"Gandi Sang-dung"	Zoomorphic form	17 × 21	
13.	"Sandhan"	Animal form	11.2 × 14.5	
14.	"Minati"	Dog	12.8 × 18.8	
15.	"Bholanath"	Figure	13.5 × 22	
16.	"Utkata-danti"		14 × 25	7.11.1936
17.	"Pandeji"	Head study	13 × 17.5	
18.	"Byasta"	Human figure	14 × 19	
19.	"Strir bon"	Female figure	13 × 18.5	
20.	"Eskul Arano"	Face of a boy	14.3 × 17	
21.	"Mejo Bau"	Female figure	17 × 21	
22.	"Neyamat Darji"	Face of a man	11 × 19.5	
23.	"Pachamba"	Female figure	11.2 × 19	
24.	"Benu"	Figure	13.5 × 23.2	
25.	"Sakal Atta"	Reclined figure	13 × 16.5	
26.	"Mokter"	Illustration for "Se"	13 × 18.2	
27.	"Adhkhana Bel"	Illustration for "Khapchhada"	12 × 17.5	
28.	"Khudiram"	Sketch of a boy	12 × 21.5	
29.	"Damodar Seth"	Man in profile-illustration for "Khapchhada"	11 × 20	6.11.1936
30.	"Pencho"	Illustration for "Khapchhada"	12.5 × 19.5	
31.	"Matilal Nandi"	Illustration for "Khapchhada"	10.6 × 15.7	
32.	"Narahari Sharma"	Illustration for "Khapchhada"	7.5 × 14.5	
33.	"Kabi Adhunik"	Illustration for "Khapchhada"	16 × 21	Bhadra,1943
34.	"Rannar sab thik"	Illustration for "Khapchada"	12 × 16	
35.	"Badsa"	Illustration for "Khapchhada"	16 × 19.5	
36.	"M.Sc."	Illustration for "Khapchada"	8 × 13	
37.	"Chhoto Bau"	Illustration for "Khapchhada"	16 × 19.5	
38.	"Sindh kata"	Illustration for "Khapchhada"	16 × 20.2	
39.	"Paltar khudu"	Illustration for "Khapchhada"	16 × 20	
40.	"Baneshwar"	Illustration for "Khapchhada"	16 × 20	
41.	"Mukh dheke"	Illustration for "Khapchhada"	16 × 20	

(Contd.)

Sl. No.	Titles	Theme	Size in cm.	Date
42.	"Neyamat darji"	Illustration for "Khapchhada"	16 × 20	
43.	"Daktar"	Illustration for "Khapchhada"	16 × 20	
44.	"Siraj"		16.2 × 25	
45.	"Alu"		17.3 × 23	
46.	"Aluke"	Mask like face	22 × 30	16.4.1940

Discussion

It is surprising to note that Rabindranath, as a painter, was first recognized in the West, mainly after his exhibitions at Paris in the year 1930. A list of exhibitions during Tagore's lifetime would justify this statement.

Table 8.48: Exhibitions of Paintings and Drawings of Rabindranath during his Lifetime.

Sl. No.	Year	Gallery	Place	Country
1.	1930, May	Galerie Pigalle	Paris	France
2.	June	City Art Gallery	Birmingham	U.K.
3.	June	India Society	London	U.K.
4.	July	Moeller's Gallery	Berlin	Germany
5.	July	Art Club of Saxony	Dresden	Germany
6.	July	Gallery Caspari	Munich	Germany
7.	August	Charlottenburg Picture Gallery	Copenhagen	Denmark
8.	August-September	Geneva	Geneva	Switzerland
9.	September	State Museum of New Western Art	Moscow	U.S.S.R.
10.	October	Doll and Richards Gallery	Boston	U.S.A.
11.	October	Museum of Fine Arts	Boston	U.S.A.
12.	December	Fifty-Sixth Street Galleries	New York	U.S.A.
13.	December	Newman Galleries	Philadelphia	U.S.A.
14.	1931 December	Town Hall	Calcutta	India
15.	1932 February	Government School of Art	Calcutta	India
16.	1933 November	Town Hall	Bombay	India
17.	1934 May	Colombo	Colombo	Ceylon
18.	October	Congress House	Madras	India
19.	1938 December	Calmann Gallery	London	U.K.
20.	1939 February	Bangiya Sahitya Parishad	Calcutta	India

Source: Rabindra-Chitrakala: Rabindrasahityer Patabhumika.

It is clear from the study that Rabindranath composed a good number of drawings and paintings in a short span of 12 years (15.3.1929—3.11.1940) on different themes, with various colour combinations. As subject Rabindranath's paintings include figure in different shapes and forms, human face, head study, landscape, birds, animals, nude etc. Every subject has its own childlike imaginary rhythmic specialty. Regarding the head study observation of sculpture Marguerite Milward after Paris exhibition is worthy to mention "Perhaps the heads attract me the most, faces of every shape, sometimes only eyes that haunt and follow me out of the dark. Here is a portrait perhaps, very soft and flat in colour, a shape of hair, oval face and smiling mouth. A dream indeed weird and beautiful."[10] We may quote Vossische Zeitung observation on Berlin exhibition dated 16.7.1930, "New visions were seized in his pictures that descend to the depth, to the origin, of which the reality of the world is only a feeble copy, reflected light. Animals play a great part in them, but not those from the zoo, but those who alarm us in black nightmares. The way Tagore coloured these monkeys, tigers, vultures and marauders, displays the educated sensitive taste of oldest culture; radish brownish yellowish tones that ate full of coloured life often contrast with the black background that plays an important part—it is the night of dream. We meet with dark harmonies of the deep mystery, from where the objects often emerge with light outlines."[11]

As a medium of painting Rabindranath used mainly ink (41.513%). But single or various combinations of pen ink, waterproof ink, water colour, crayon, poster colour, pastel, pencil, vegetable colour etc. used mainly on paper (96.88%). Whatever medium Rabindranath used "his colours are scattered through nature."[12] Regarding role of lines with different medium in paintings Rabindranath had deep feelings as he narrated in his speech in London India society "It interests me deeply to watch how line find their life and character, as their connection with each other develops in varied cadences, and how they begin to speak in gesticulations. I can imagine the universe to be a universe of lines".[13]

Rabindranath signed in 903 paintings (60.903%) in different languages (pre-dominantly in Bengali 903, i.e. 94.26%), different combinations and in different types and style. Out of signed paintings he signed "Rabindra" in Bengali in 571 paintings (63.23%) and "Sri Rabindra" in 299 (33.11%) paintings. According to Tagore biographer Prabhatkumar Rabindranath stopped writing "Sri" in August 1932. But he used to write "Sri Rabindra" in paintings. Later on Rabindranath stopped writing "Sri" in his paintings also.[14] This statement can be justified as according to available dates Rabindranath produced most of the paintings after 1932. Rabindranath signed in majority of his paintings (60.903%), but gave dates only to 473 paintings only 30.070 per cent. This creates a great hindrance in determining chronological index on paintings in Tagoreana. But one interesting finding comes from the available dates that Rabindranath painted 2, 3 paintings in a day quite a number of times, even four pictures (6.1.1934, 7.11.1938, 20.7.1939) and five pictures in a day in two occasions (25.10.1934, 7.11.1935) and six paintings once (28.6.1938).

During study of paintings it was also observed that Rabindranath used various sizes of canvas for his paintings. Largest size of painting is 70.5 × 78 Centimetre (cm), largest breath of painting is 60.8 × 90.4 cm. Similarly, smallest size and breath of paintings are 8 × 3 cm, lowest length 3.5 × 48.5 cm respectively. Maximum number of paintings 37 are in the size of 25.5 × 35.5 cm.

Conclusion

It is very difficult to explain why at the age of sixty seven Rabindranath started painting as a non-verbal medium of expression. Many guesses are there, such as declining reputation, conflicting ideologies, fear of death etc. The statistical analysis shows the variety of colour, theme, size, date etc. of Rabindranath's paintings and drawings, but mere statistical analysis cannot reveal the inner insight of painting. We may note Nandalal Bose's observation in this respect "majority of the artists begin the creative processes with the subject or idea... But

Rabindranath, it seems, often begins creating even before the subject has taken any conscious form in his mind. This might easily lead one to suppose that mere craftsmanship or mere architectural design or the mere effect of colours were his end, but when the picture is complete we discover all the essential constituents of a work of art in it, all blended in one subject and pervaded by that rhythm of life which the hand of genius alone can impart. That is why his paintings are always real, though rarely realistic."[15] Actually, it is not realistic but "his art is mainly symbolic—whether it is poetry, or music, or dance, or painting... Even the portraits were the symbols of abstract qualities."[16] Yeast's opinion on Tagoreana can be applicable to Rabindranath's paintings and drawings also. "Most persons write so that if you were to detach a sentence from its context, it would have no meaning. With Tagore's writing, however, it is just the other way round. Almost any sentence will stand by itself—almost any clause. The more you study his compositions, the more significant do they become. They grow upon you."[17] A more realistic view may be "his artistic language and skills were limited, but within those limitations he created a very personal form of modernism with the power to disturb and astonish."[18]

Notes and References

1. Bandyopadhyay, Somendranath. (1982), *Rabindra-chitrakala: Rabindrasahitytyer Patabhumika*. Calcutta: Dey's Publishing, p. 18.
2. It is difficult to access the actual number of Rabindranath's paintings and drawings as many may be in the personal collection in India and abroad. There are 1573 paintings and drawings in Rabindra Bhavana, Visva-Bharati, about 100 at National Gallery of Modern Art, New Delhi, 45 at Rabindra Bharati Museum, Calcutta, 19 at Dartinghall Trust, 32 are held by the Academy of Fine Arts. A thorough bibliometric study requires immense time-consuming research. Here a study on the collection of 1573 paintings and drawings held by Visva-Bharati has been made.
3. Tagore, Rabindranath. 1958, *On the Edges of Time*. Cacutta: Orient Longman.

4. Letter of Rabindranath to William Rothenstein. (March 1930). Preserved in Tagore Museum (Rabindra Bhavana), Santiniketan.
5. Tagore, Rabindranath. (1961,) My pictures. In *Rabindranath Tagore on Art and Aesthetics.* Ed. Neogy, Pritwish. New Delhi: Orient Longman, pp. 97-98.
6. Lago, Mary, M. (1978), *Letters of William Rothenstein and Rabindranath Tagore 1911-1941.* Harvard: Harvard University Press.
7. Mitter, Parha. 2007, *The Triumph of Modernism: Indian Artists and the Avant-garde: 1922-1947.* New Delhi: Oxford University Press, p. 69.
8. Tagore, Rabindranath. (1961), My pictures. In *Rabindranath Tagore on Art and Aesthetics.* Ed. Neogy, Tagore, Rabindranath. My pictures. In *Rabindranath Tagore on Art and Aesthetics.* Ed. Neogy, Pritwish. New Delhi: Orient Longman, p. 104.
9. Printed over *Visva-Bharati News: Birthday No. Cover,* 2(11) (1934).
10. Muillward, R.M. (1930) Rabindranath Tagore in Paris. *Modern Review.* 11: 545.
11. Bandyopadhyay, Somendranath. (1982), *Rabindra-chitrakala: Rabindrasahitytyer Patabhumika.* Calcutta: Dey's Publishing, p. 140.
12. Tagore, Abanindranath. (1947). *Exhibitions of Paintings and Drawings of Rabindranath Tagore.* In *Exhibition catalogue.* Ed. Majumdar Kamal.
13. Rafique Ahmad. (1996), *Rabindranather chitrasilpa.* Dhaka: National Academy of Fine and Performing Arts, p. 140.
14. Mukhopadhyaya, Prabhatkumar. (1961), *Rabindrajibani O Rabindra Sahitya Prabashak,* Vol. 3. Calcutta: Visva-Bharati Granthan Vibhaga, p. 247.
15. Bose, Nandalal (1936) The Paintings of Rabindranath. *Visva-Bharati Quarterly,* 14(1): 31.
16. Bagchi, Radhacharan. (1962), *Rabindranath Tagore as a Painter, In Homage from Visva-Bharati.* Ed. Sengupta, Santosh Chandra. Calcutta: Visva-Bharati Granthan Vibhaga, p. 200.
17. Singh, Nihar. Tagore's conversion with Yeats in Dublin, *Calcutta Municipal Gazette.* 13th September, 1941.
18. Chaudhuri, Amit (2006) Two Giant brothers. *London Review of Books, 28*(8): 27-30.

9

Rabindranath Tagore

A Bibliometric Portrait

Introduction

Rabindranath Tagore (1861-1941), the fourteenth child of Debendranath Tagore (1817-1906) and Sarada Devi (1826-1875), was born on 7th May, 1861 in the ancestral mansion of the Tagore family in Jorasanko, in central Calcuta. Rabindranath Tagore, the myriad-minded poet and writer composed his first poem at the age of eight and by the end of his life at the age of eighty, he has created literature in all forms like poetry, short stories, novels, essays; initiated and edited various journals; prepared Bengali textbooks, penned thousands of letters; and crossing the age of seventy he created more than two thousand paintings and drawings.[1] Rabindranath, the writer of two National anthems, has composed more than two thousand songs[2] known as *Rabindra Sangit* that have become a symbol of cultural ethos of both India and Bangladesh. Tagore's literary journey starts with the publication of the first poem signed in his own name *Hindu Melār Upahār* (The Gift of Hindu Mela). The poet read this poem at the 9th Annual Conference of Hindu Mela on 12th February, 1875. The poem was of 22 stanzas with 88 lines. It was published in the *Prabashi Patrika* in 1338 (B.S.) Magh issue[3] and first verse narrative *Banaphul* (The Wild Flower) was published in *Jnanankur* and *Pratibimba.* The last birthday of Rabindranath (7th May, 1941) is marked with the publication of three books, one in verse called *Janmadine* (On my Birthday), one comprising short stories, *Galpasalpa* and the English version of *Chhelebela* (Boyhood days). The first verse narrative *Banaphul* is a long narrative poem in eight cantos, running over 1600 lines. It is the story of a young girl

Kamala who was brought up by her father in a solitary retreat in the Himalayas.[4]

Rabindranath had no formal institutional educational degree, but his family's piety, honesty, love of nature and sense of beauty made a great impression on him. Ramananda Chatterjee, a renowned literary personality of Bengal referred the family as "the most gifted in Bengal in the realms of religion, philosophy, literature, music, painting and the histrionic art."[5] Rabindranath himself acknowledged "one great advantage which I enjoyed in my younger days was the literary and artistic atmosphere which prevailed in our house."[6]

Rabindranath received the Nobel Prize for literature on 13th November, 1913 for *Gitanjali* (Song Offerings) published by Indian Society of London on 1st November, 1912. The recommendation to Swedish Academy came from another Nobel laureate Werner von Heidenstam. He wrote "They [songs] gave me hours of intense enjoyment; it was like drinking the water of a fresh, clear spring...There is nothing in his work that is controversial and offensive, nothing vain, worldly and petty, and if ever a poet may be said to possess the qualities that make him entitled to the Nobel prize, it is he."[7]

Tagore's intellectual output, Tagoreana covers all aspects of human life such as society, religion, aesthetics, education, rural reconstruction, nationalism, internationalism in all forms of literature as well as drawings and paintings. Bibliometric study on different segments of his literary creation such as songs[8], letters[9], Nobel Prize winning book of poems *Gitanjali* (Song Offerings)[10] etc. have been carried out. But no study has been carried out considering his total intellectual output in different literary forms particularly from the point of view of information science. But quantitative and qualitative studies of productivity of a creator with proper graphical representation help to analyse and understand his/her contribution in proper perspective.

A good number of scientometric studies on the works of Nobel Laureate[11-19] scientists have been carried out. Besides, studies have been reported on the works of other eminent scientists[20-27] to draw their scientometric portrait. But for quantitative analysis of publication profile of social scientists, bibliometric techniques[28-29] had been applied. Here also bibliometric technique have been applied to measure production output of the Nobel Laureate Rabindranath Tagore.

Objectives of the Study

- To measure quantitatively Rabindranath's contribution to literature;
- To find out year-wise growth of publications;
- To identify literary-form-wise distribution of publications; and
- To identify core communication channels preferred by Rabindranath for the publication of his short stories.

Methodology

Creation of bibliometric profile requires quantitative and qualitative documentation of an individual scholar. Its graphic representation facilitates easy and clear perception of a scientist. A comprehensive bibliography consisting of publications of Bengali and English books were compiled in chronological order. The bibliography includes all publications of his lifetime (n = 199) and also posthumous publications (n = 36) in Bengali language as well as books in English language (n = 52). The year of publication has been considered as contribution in a particular year. Rabindranath wrote 95 short stories and used different communicational channels for publication. Short stories by the poet have been considered as scientific communication as they carry messages on social, political, economic, cultural aspects of the society. The books and short stories are the source of this study. Items appeared in the bibliographical fields of publication were inputted and analysed. The present study is delimited to published books (including books on songs, letters, paintings etc.) and short stories only.

Results and Discussion

Rabindranath published 199 books in a span of 64 years (1878-1941). The number of posthumous publications totals 39 (1941-1979). Visva-Bharati published all unpublished works of Rabindranath particularly collection of letters, essays, lectures as individual volume after his death. The grand total of the publications is 235 as shown in Table 9.1. It may be noted that during his lifetime the author did not publish any Bengali book in the years 1879, 1890, 1898, 1902, 1904, 1913, 1915, and 1924. It looks unbelievable that the year in which he won the Nobel Prize, his mighty pen did not yield any Bengali book! The maximum number of books (N = 9) came out in 1907, 1908 and 1936 when he was 46, 47 and 75 years old. It may be noted that in his seventies he ventured upon another field of art, i.e. painting and contributed profusely. Despite his profound engagement in painting, his literary activity did not diminish at all rather increased. In his seventies he produced as many as 55 books. In no other decade of his life he could produce so many books. This period was the most productive period of Tagore's life. This may be a rare phenomenon which only further studies can corroborate.

Table 9.1: Chronological distribution of Bengali Books

Author's age	*Year*	*No. of Publications*	*Cumulative Total*	*Publishing Age*
17	1878	1	1	1
19	1880	1	2	2
20	1881	4	6	3
21	1882	2	8	4
22	1883	3	11	5
23	1884	5	16	6
24	1885	3	19	7
25	1886	1	20	8
26	1887	2	22	9
27	1888	2	24	10
28	1889	1	25	11
30	1891	1	26	12
31	1892	2	28	13
32	1893	2	30	14
33	1894	5	35	15
34	1895	1	36	16
35	1896	2	38	17
36	1897	2	40	18
38	1899	1	41	19
39	1900	5	46	20
40	1901	3	49	21
42	1903	3	52	22
44	1905	2	54	23
45	1906	3	57	24
46	1907	9	66	25
47	1908	9	75	26
48	1909	6	81	27
49	1910	5	86	28
50	1911	1	87	29
51	1912	7	94	30
53	1914	5	99	31

(Contd. ...)

Author's age	Year	No. of Publications	Cumulative Total	Publishing Age
55	1916	7	106	32
56	1917	1	107	33
57	1918	2	109	34
58	1919	1	110	35
59	1920	2	112	36
60	1921	1	113	37
61	1922	3	116	38
62	1923	1	117	39
64	1925	3	120	40
65	1926	5	125	41
66	1927	2	127	42
67	1928	1	128	43
68	1929	7	135	44
69	1930	1	136	45
70	1931	7	143	46
71	1932	4	147	47
72	1933	8	155	48
73	1934	3	158	49
74	1935	3	161	50
75	1936	9	170	51
76	1937	5	175	52
77	1938	6	181	53
78	1939	4	185	54
79	1940	6	191	55
80	1941	5	196	56
80	1941*	3	199	56
81	1942	3	202	57
82	1943	3	205	58
84	1945	2	207	60
87	1948	2	209	61
90	1951	3	212	62
91	1952	1	213	63
93	1954	2	215	64
94	1955	1	216	65
95	1956	1	217	66
96	1957	1	218	67
98	1959	1	219	68
99	1960	2	221	69
101	1962	1	222	70
102	1963	3	225	71
103	1964	1	226	72
104	1965	1	227	73
105	1966	1	228	74
106	1967	1	229	75
107	1968	1	230	76
111	1972	1	231	77
113	1974	2	233	78
116	1977	1	234	79
118	1979	1	235	80

* Post-1941 books are posthumous publications.

Tagore's productivity is graphically presented in Fig. 9.1 for his lifetime publications and in Fig. 9.2 for posthumous publications.

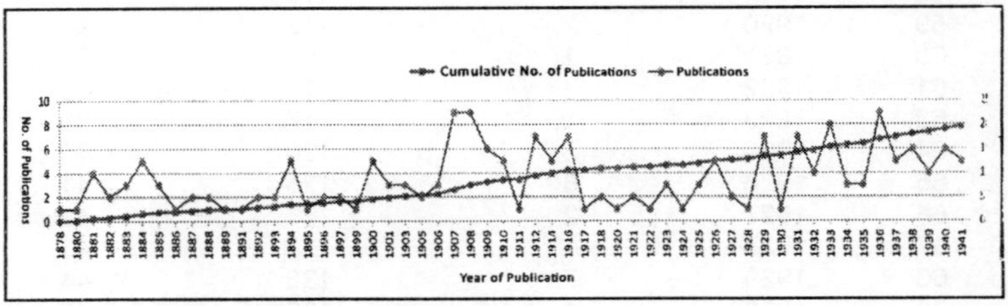

Fig. 9.1: Productivity Output (up to 1941)

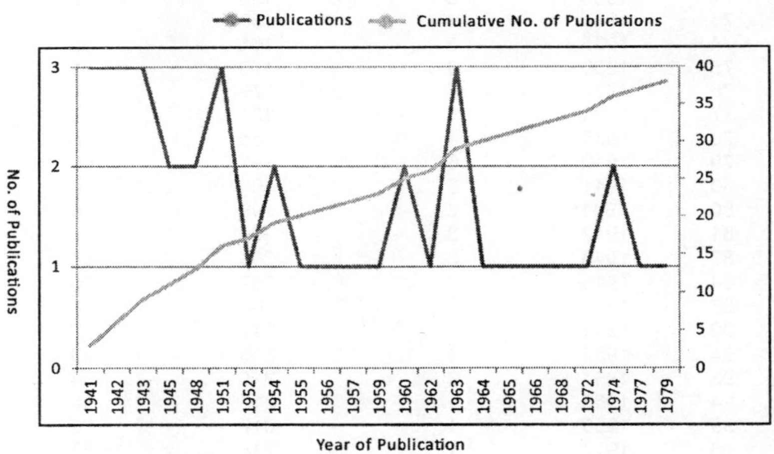

Fig.9.2: Productivity Output (upto 1941)

The productivity coefficient could be obtained by the simple formula of 50 percentile age per total productivity age. Fifty percentile age is the number of years during which 50 per cent of the papers (books in this study) were published starting from the year of publication of the first paper. Productivity age on the other hand is the count from the year in which first paper by an author was published till the last year of publication.[30] Tagore's productivity coefficient for Bengali books is 0.84 (where fifty percentile ages is 67 and publishing age as 80 including posthumous publications).

Rabindranath created his literary works embracing all literary forms. A literary form-wise distribution of his intellectual output is given in Table 9.2 and Fig. 9.3. It is seen that his books on essays top the list (N = 47), followed by drama (46), verse (44), songs/poems (22), novels and short stories (13 each), and so on.

Table 9.2: Literary form-wise distribution of Bengali books

Literary form	*Total Number of Books*	*FPY*	*LPY*	*%*
Verse	44	1878	1965	18.72
Drama	46	1881	1979	19.58
Letters	21	1881	1974	08.94
Novel	13	1883	1934	05.53
Essays	47	1883	1968	20.00
Songs/Poems	22	1884	1954	09.36
Travelogues	7	1891	1963	02.98
Comedy	5	1892	1948	02.13
Short Stories	13	1894	1940	05.53
Address	9	1907	1977	03.83
Textbook	4	1910	1931	01.70
Autobiography	2	1912	1940	00.85
Drawing and Paintings	2	1940	1951	00.85
Total	**235**			**100.00**

FPY=First Publication Year, LPY= Last Publication Year

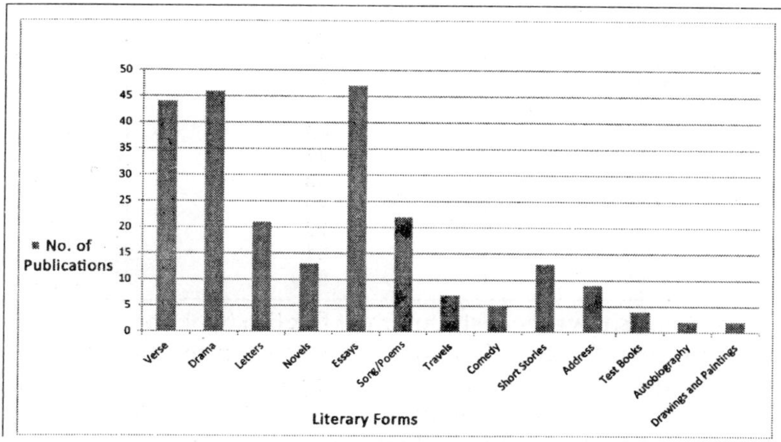

Fig.3: Literary form-wise distribution of productivity

Essays and Other Works in English

Rabindranath predominately wrote in Bengali, but there are 52 books in English to his credit produced in a span of 21 years (1912-1941) (Table 9.3). His writings in English are mostly translations of his own work in Bengali. Only *Poems of Kabir,* a translation of poems by Kabir is an exception. Like Bengali books Tagore's writing in English covers different literary forms. Table 9.3 shows that five English books appeared in 1913, 1917, and 1921. Prior to 1913, only one book was translated. Tagore's winning of Nobel Prize in 1913 seems to have inspired the poet to go for more translations. The English translations of his book continued till the end of his life.

Table 9.3: Year-wise publication of English books

Age	*Year*	*No. of Publications*	*Cumulative Total*	*Publishing Age*
51	1912	1	1	1
52	1913	5	6	2
53	1914	3	9	3
55	1916	3	12	4
56	1917	5	17	5
57	1918	4	21	6
58	1919	2	23	7
60	1921	5	28	8
61	1922	2	30	9
62	1923	1	31	10
63	1924	3	34	11
64	1925	4	38	12
67	1928	4	42	13
68	1929	1	43	14
70	1931	2	45	15
72	1932	2	47	16
74	1935	1	48	17
75	1936	1	49	18
76	1937	1	50	19
79	1940	1	51	20
80	1941	1	52	21

Table 9.4 shows the distribution of English books according to literary forms. Expectedly books of poems top the list with 15, followed by short stories and dramas (7 each), essays (5), and so on.

The percentage of Bengali *vis-a-vis* English publications of Tagore (1878-1979) is graphically shown in Fig. 9.4. As more books of Tagore are being translated, it is expected that the percentage of English books will rise.

Table 9.4: Literary form-wise distribution of English books

Literary form	*Number of Books*	*FPY*	*LPY*	*%*
Poem	15	1912	1936	28.85
Short Stories	7	1913	1941	13.46
Essays	5	1913	1923	09.62
Drama	7	1913	1925	13.46
Autobiography	1	1917	—	01.92
Address	7	1917	1937	13.46
Novel	3	1919	1924	05.77
Letters	3	1921	1935	05.77
Compilation	3	1928	1929	05.77
Autobiography	1	1940	—	01.92
Total	**52**			**100.00**

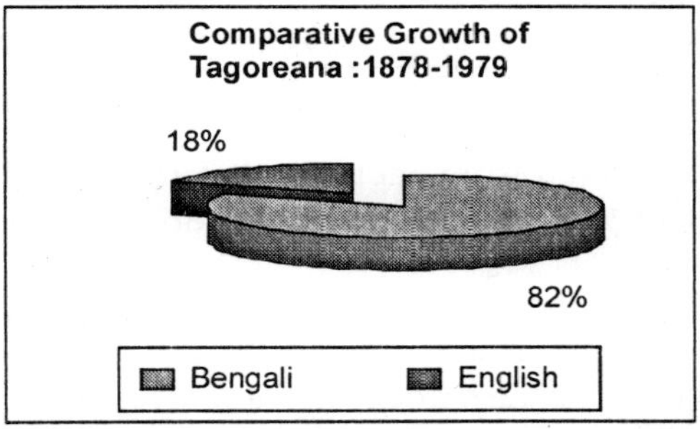

Fig. 9.4: Comparative productivity of Bengali and English books

Short Stories

The art of short story writing has in recent times received a great deal of attention in literary circle. But when Rabindranath started writing short stories the practice had not been fully established. Through its brevity, the short story subjected the writer to a discipline and for a period Rabindranath welcomed this discipline for his objective writing. A study of Rabindranath's short stories in the chronological order would help study pattern and change in joint family life, outside family ties, social structure etc. and also change of elements of dialogue from third person narratives to dialogue-based writings. Rabindranath wrote 95[31] short stories of which 91 were published in 16 communication channels as shown in Table 9.5. It can be observed from Table 9.5 that *Sādhanā* and *Bhāratī* were his most preferred journals to place his short stories.

Table 9.5: Channel-wise scattering of short stories (SS)

Sl.No.	Journals	No. of SS	FPY	LPY	%
1.	Bhāratī	16	1878	1911	17.58
2.	Nabajiban	01	1884	1884	01.10
3.	Bālak	01	1885	1885	01.10
4.	Hitavādi	07	1891	1891	07.69
5.	Sādhanā	36	1891	1895	39.56
6.	Sakhā o Sāthi	01	1895	1895	01.10
7.	Pradeep	02	1900	1900	02.20
8.	Bangadarshan	03	1902	1904	03.30
9.	Prabāshi	06	1907	1941	06.59
10.	Subajputra	10	1914	1917	10.98
11.	Chotogalpa	01	1933	1933	01.10
12.	Anandabazār (Puja Sankha)	03	1939	1941	03.30
13.	Sanibārer Chithi	01	1939	1939	01.10
14.	Desh	01	1939	1939	01.10
15.	Visva-Bhārati Patrikā	01	1942	1942	01.10
16.	Ritupatra	01	1955	1955	01.10
	Total	**91**	**1887**	**1955**	**100.00**

It can be observed from Table 9.6 that 1891 and 1892 are the most productive year in terms of publication of short stories by Tagore.

Productivity coefficient for short stories of Rabindranath is 9/28, i.e. 0.32 (where 9 is 50 percentile age and 28 is total productivity age). Publication density[32] is the ratio of total number of papers published to the total number of journals in which papers were published. Publication density of Rabindranath's short stories is found to be 91/16, i.e. 5.69. Publication concentration on the other hand is the ratio in percentage of the channels having half of the papers published to the total number of journals in which those papers were published. Tagore published his short stories in 16 channels among which two channels, namely *Bhāratī* (n = 16) and *Sādhanā* (n = 36) covers more than half of the short stories. Hence, publication concentration of short stories would be : 2/16 × 100, i.e. 12.5.

Conclusion

In case of literature what matters is the depth of knowledge; wisdom expressed in writings not the numbers. The romantic touches reflected in the novels of Rabindranath come from His rapport with the beauty and mystery in nature deeply rooted in social, family and individual life. It is desirable to see the novels

Table 9.6: Year-wise publication of Short Stories

Age of T	*Year*	*No. of Publications*	*Cumulative Total*	*Publishing Age*
17	1878	1	1	1
18	1879	1	2	2
23	1884	2	4	3
24	1885	1	5	4
30	1891	12	17	5
31	1892	12	29	6
32	1893	7	36	7
33	1894	7	43	8
34	1895	6	49	9
37	1898	7	56	10
39	1900	5	61	11
40	1901	1	62	12
41	1902	2	64	14
43	1904	1	65	15
46	1907	1	66	16
50	1911	2	68	17
53	1914	7	75	18
56	1917	3	78	19
64	1925	1	79	20
67	1928	1	80	21
68	1929	2	82	22
72	1933	1	83	23
78	1939	3	86	24
79	1940	1	87	25
80	1941	2	89	26
81	1942	1	90	27
94	1955	1	91	28

as a part of changing social history – reflection of society. In his short stories also problems relating to personal, familial, social, etc. are not denied, but presented in an aesthetically valid universe. These reflections can never be measured with mere statistical indicators.

While considering the literary productivity of Rabindranath one should not forget that Rabindranath not only expressed his vision on society, education, rural development, religion, in his numerous writings, but also tried to give it a concrete shape with the establishment of his experimental school at Santiniketan and rural reconstruction programme at Sriniketan. He wished to "bring to the village health and knowledge, wealth and peace in which to live, wealth of time in which to work and to rest and enjoy."[33] Reform of education and regeneration of villages were the major tasks of his life.

References

1. Ray, P.P. (2012), *Tagore in Print: A Comparative study before and after expiry of Copyright.* New Delhi: Concept Publishing Co. (P.) Ltd., pp. 87-108.
2. Ray, P.P. and Sen, B.K., (2012), Rabindrasangit (songs of Rabindranath Tagore): a bibliometric study. *SRELS Journal of Information Management.* 49(4): 343-358.
3. Bandyopadhyaya, B., *Rabindra granthaparichaya (1878-1943).* Calcutta: Sahitya Niketan, 1349 (B.S.), p. 28.
4. Kripalani, K., (1980), *Rabindranath Tagore: A Biography.* Calcutta: Visva Bharati Granthan Vibhaga, p. 66.
5. Chatterjee, R., (1931), Rabindranath Tagore, *Modern Review.* 50.6: 675.
6. Tagore, Rabindranath. (2017), *Reminiscences.* London: MacMillan & Co., pp. 116-117.
7. Robinson, A., (1989), *The Art of Rabindranath Tagore.* Calcutta: Rupa, p. 33.
8. Ray, P.P. (2012), Rabindrasangit (song of Rabindranath Tagore): a bibliometric study. *SRELS Journal of Information Management.* 49(4): 343-358.
9. Ray, P.P. and Sen, B.K. (2012), Letter Correspondence of Rabindranath Tagore: a study. *Annals of Library and Information Studies.* 59 (2): 122-127.
10. Ray, P.P. (2012), *Gitanjali* (Song Offerings): a bibliometric study. *SRELS Journal of Information Management.* 49(6): 601-613.
11. Gupta, D.K. (1999) Chandrasekhar: winner of the Nobel Prize for physics: a citation analysis of his work. *Annals of Library and Information Studies.* 30 (14): 177-184.
12. Kademani, B.S.; Kalyane, V.L. and Jange, S. (1999) Scientometric portrait of Nobel Laureate Dorothy Crowfoot Hodgkin. *Scientometrics.* 45 (2): 233-250.
13. Kademani, B.S.; Kalyane, V.L. and Kademani, A.B. (1994) Scientometric portrait of Nobel Laureate Dr. C.V. Raman. *Indian Journal of Information, Library and Society.* 7 (3-4): 215-249.
14. Kademani, B.S.; Kalyane, V.L. and Kademani, A.B. (1996) Scientometric portrait of Nobel Laureate S. Chandrasekhar. *JISSI: The International Journal of Scientometrics and Informetrics.* 2 (2-3): 119-135.
15. Kademani, B.S.; Kalyane, V.L. and Kumar, V. (2002) Scientometric portrait of Nobel Laureate Harold W. Kroto. *SRELS Journal of Information Management.* 39(4): 409-434.
16. Kademani, B.S.; Kalyane, V.L. and Kumar, V. (2002) Scientometric portrait of Nobel Laureate Ahmed Hassan Zewail. *Malaysian Journal of Library and Information Science.* 6(2): 53-70.
17. Kalyane, V.L. and Kademani, B.S. (1997) Scientometric portrait of Barbara McClintock: the Nobel Laureate in Physiology. *Kelpro Bulletin.* 1 (1): 3-14.

18. Kalyane, V.L. and Sen, B.K. (1996) Scientometric portrait of Nobel Laureate Pierre-Gilles de Gennes. *Malaysian Journal of Library and Information Science.* 1 (2): 1326.
19. Koganuramath, M.M. *et al.*, (2004), Physics Nobel Laureate Wolfgang Ketterle: A scientometric portrait. *Malaysian Journal of Library and Information Science.* 9 (2): 35-61.
20. Hazarika, T.S.; Sarma, D. and Sen, B.K. (2010) Scientometric portrait of Nayana Nanda Borthakur: a biometeorologist. *Annals of Library and Information Studies.* 57 (1): 21-32.
21. Kademani, B.S. and Kalyane, V.L. (1996) Bibliometric indicators of publication productivity analysis of an individual scientist. *JISSI: The International Journal of Scientometrics and Informetrics.* 2 (4): 49-58.
22. Kademani, B.S.; Kalyane, V.L. and Balakrishnan, M.R. (1994) Scientometric portrait of P. K. Iyengar. *Library Science.* 31 (4): 155-176.
23. Kademani, B.S.; Kalyane, V.L. and Kademani, A.B. (1996) Scientometric portrait of Sir K.S. Krishnan. *Indian Journal of Information Library and Society.* 9 (1-2): 125-150.
24. Kademani, B.S.; Kalyane, V.S. and Kumar, V. (2000), Scientometric portrait of Vikram Ambalal Sarabhai: a citation analysis. *SRELS Journal of Information Management.* 37 (2): 107-132.
25. Kademani, B.S.; Surwase, G. and Kumar, V. (2009), Bhabha Scattering: a Scientometric View. *DESIDOC Journal of Library & Information Technology.* 29 (4): 3-11.
26. Kalyane, V.L. and Kademani, B.S. (1995), Scientometric Portrait of R. Chidambaram: a publication productivity analysis. *Journal of Information Sciences.* 5 (3): 101-140.
27. Kalyane, V.L. and Munnolli, S.S. (1995), Scientometric Portrait of T.S. West. *Scientometrics.* 33 (2): 233-256.
28. Sinha, S.C. and Ullah, M.F. (1994), Information profile of an Indian bibliometrician: Bibliometric study of Dr. I.N. Sengupta's Publications. *Indian Journal of Information, Library and Society.* 7 (3-4): 250-261.
29. Tiew, W.S. (1999), Khoo Kay Kim: Professor of Malaysian History: a bibliometric study. *Malaysian Journal of Library and Information Science.* 4 (2): 47-57.
30. Sen, S.K. and Gan, S.K. (1990), Bibliometrics: concept and application in the study of productivity of scientists. *International Forum on Information and Documentation.* 15.3: 13-21.
31. Tagore, Rabindranath. (1999), *Galpaguccha.* Calcutta: Visva Bharati Granthan Vibhaga.
32. Vinkler, P. (1990), *Bibliometric Analysis of Publication Activity of a Scientific Research Institute.* Amsterdam: Elsevier, pp. 309-334.
33. Tagore, Rabindranath. *Jivansmriti.* Calcutta: Visva Bharati Granthan Vibhaga, 1405(B.S), p. 13.

Index